SRA
Open Court Reading

Level 2 • Book 1

Sharing Stories
•
Kindness
•
Look Again

Level 2 • Book 1

— PROGRAM AUTHORS —

Carl Bereiter Michael Pressley Joe Campione

Marilyn Jager Adams Marsha Roit Iva Carruthers

Marlene Scardamalia Jan Hirshberg Gerald H. Treadway, Jr.

Anne McKeough

A Division of The McGraw·Hill Companies

Columbus, Ohio

Acknowledgments

Grateful acknowledgement is given to the following publishers and copyright owners for permissions granted to reprint selections from their publications. All possible care has been taken to trace ownership and secure permission for each selection included. In case of any errors or omissions, the Publisher will be pleased to make suitable acknowledgements in future editions.

SHARING STORIES

"Ant and the Three Little Figs" from MY BROTHER, ANT by Betsy Byars, text copyright © 1996 by Betsy Byars. Used by permission of Viking Penguin, an imprint of Penguin Putnam Books for Young Readers, a division of Penguin Putnam, Inc. "Ant and the Three Little Figs" from MY BROTHER, ANT by Betsy Byars, illustrated by Marc Simont, copyright © 1996 by Marc Simont. Used by permission of Viking Penguin, an imprint of Penguin Putnam Books for Young Readers, a division of Penguin Putnam, Inc.

"Books to the Ceiling" from WHISKERS AND RHYMES by Arnold Lobel. COPYRIGHT © 1985 BY ARNOLD LOBEL. Used by permission of HarperCollins Publishers.

COME BACK, JACK! Copyright © 1993 Catherine and Laurence Anholt. Reproduced by permission of Candlewick Press Inc., Cambridge, MA, on behalf of Walker Books Ltd., London.

"My Book" from Somebody Catch My Homework by David L. Harrison. Text copyright © 1993 by David L. Harrison. Published by Boyds Mills Press, Inc. Reprinted by permission.

THE LIBRARY by Sarah Stewart, illustrated by David Small. Text copyright © 1995 by Sarah Stewart. Illustrations copyright © 1995 by David Small. Reprinted by permission of Farrar, Straus & Giroux, LLC.

STORY HOUR-STARRING MEGAN! text and illustrations © 1992 by Julie Brillhart. Reprinted by permission of the author.

TOMAS AND THE LIBRARY LADY text copyright © 1997 by Pat Mora. Illustrations copyright © 1997 by Raul Colon. Reprinted by arrangement with Random House Children's Books, a division of Random House, Inc., New York, New York. All rights reserved.

KINDNESS

From MUSHROOM IN THE RAIN. Text copyright © 1974 by Mirra Ginsburg, illustrations copyright © 1974 by Jose Aruego and Arianne Dewey. Reprinted with permission of Simon & Schuster Books for Young Readers, Simon & Schuster Children's Publishing Division. All rights reserved.

From THE ELVES AND SHOEMAKER retold by Freya Littledale, illustrated by Brinton Turkle. Copyright ©1975 by Freya Littledale and Brinton Turkle. Reprinted by permission of ScholasticInc.

THE PAPER CRANE TEXT COPYRIGHT © 1985 BY MOLLY BANG. Used by permission of HarperCollins Publishers.

From BUTTERFLY HOUSE by Eve Bunting, illustrated by Greg Shed. Published by Scholastic Press, a division of Scholastic Inc. Text copyright © 1999 by Edward D. Bunting and Anne E. Bunting Family Trust, illustrations copyright © 1999 by Greg Shed. Reprinted by permission.

From CORDUROY by Don Freeman, copyright © 1968 by Don Freeman. Used by permission of Viking Penguin, an imprint of Penguin Putnam Books for Young Readers, a division of Penguin Putnam Inc.

"April Medicine" from GINGERBREAD DAYS by Joyce Carol Thomas. TEXT COPYRIGHT © 1995 BY JOYCE CAROL THOMAS. ILLUSTRATIONS COPYRIGHT © 1995 BY FLOYD COOPER. Used by permission of HarperCollins Publishers.

From THE STORY OF THREE WHALES Text © Copyright 1998 by Giles Whittell, illustrations © 1998 by Patrick Benson. Reprinted with permission of Gareth Stevens Publishing. All rights reserved.

From CINDERELLA, text copyright © 1977 by Charles Perrault. Reprinted with permission of Flammarion. All rights reserved.

CAMOUFLAGE

From I SEE ANIMALS HIDING by Jim Arnosky. Copyright © 1995 by Jim Arnosky. Reprinted by permission of Scholastic Inc.

THEY THOUGHT THEY SAW HIM TEXT COPYRIGHT © 1996 BY CRAIG KEE STRETE. ILLUSTRATIONS COPYRIGHT © 1996 BY JOSE ARUEGO AND ARIANE DEWEY. Used by permission of HarperCollins Publishers.

"The Chameleon" from A CHILD'S BESTIARY, by John Gardner (New York; Alfred A. Knopf, 1977). Copyright © 1977 by Boskydell Artists Ltd. Reprinted by permission of Georges Borchardt, Inc. for the Estate of John Gardner.

From HUNGRY LITTLE HARE, text copyright © 1998 by Howard Goldsmith, illustrations copyright © 1998 by Denny Bond. Reprinted with permission of Learning Triangle Press, an imprint of The McGraw-Hill Companies. All rights reserved.

From HOW TO HIDE AN OCTAPUS & OTHER SEA CREATURES by Ruth Heller, copyright © 1985. Used by permission of Grosset & Dunlap, an imprint of Penguin Putnam Books for Young Readers, a division of Penguin Putnam Inc.

HOW THE GUINEA FOWL GOT HER SPOTS by Barbara Knutson. Copyright 1990 by Barbara Knutson. Published by Carolrhoda Books, Inc. a division of the Lerner Publishing Group. Used by permission of the publisher. All rights reserved.

Animal Camouflage by Janet McDonnell, copyright 1998 © by The Child's World ®, Chanhassen Minnesota. Reprinted by permission of copyright holder.

www.sra4kids.com

SRA/McGraw-Hill

A Division of The McGraw·Hill Companies

Send all inquiries to:
SRA/McGraw-Hill
8787 Orion Place
Columbus, Ohio 43240-4027

Printed in the United States of America.

ISBN 0-07-569244-9

2 3 4 5 6 7 8 9 RRW 04 03 02

— Program Authors —

Carl Bereiter, Ph.D.
University of Toronto

Marilyn Jager Adams, Ph.D.
BBN Technologies

Michael Pressley, Ph.D.
University of Notre Dame

Marsha Roit, Ph.D.
National Reading Consultant

Anne McKeough, Ph.D.
University of Toronto

Jan Hirshberg, Ed.D.
Reading Specialist

Marlene Scardamalia, Ph.D.
University of Calgary

Joe Campione, Ph.D.
University of California at Berkeley

Iva Carruthers, Ph.D.
Northeastern Illinois University

Gerald H. Treadway, Jr., Ed.D.
San Diego State University

Table of Contents

Table of Contents

Table of Contents

Sharing Stories

How do you share stories with your friends? What if they are too far away to talk to? Do you write to them? How can you learn new stories? Reading and writing can help us share stories with others.

Stories for Young Readers

Ant and the Three Little Figs

Betsy Byars

illustrated by Marc Simont

Ant said, "Read me a story."

I like to read.

I said, "Okay."

Ant sat down by me.

I opened the book

and began to read.

"Once upon a time

there were three little figs."

Ant sat up.

14

He said, "No! That is not right.

It's pigs. Three little PIGS.

Say PIGS."

I am easy to get along with.

I said, "Pigs."

The Ant leaned back.

He said, "Now read the story."

I read: "Once upon a time

there were three little bananas."

Ant said, "No! Don't do that!

Read the story right.

It's pigs.

Look at the picture.

There's a pig.

There's a pig.

There's a pig.

Three pigs!"

"Oh, all right. Pigs.

Once upon a time

there were three little—"

"Pigs," Ant said quickly.

"Who is reading this—

you or me?" I asked.

"You are," Ant said,

"but you have to say pigs."

"And you have to let me read.

Once upon a time

there were three little—"

I stopped and waited.

The Ant waited, too.

Finally he said,

"This is your last chance.

If you don't say pigs, I'm leaving."

I said, "Oh, all right.

Once upon a time

there were three little pigs. . . ."

Ant got down from the chair.

I said, "Where are you going, Ant?

I read it right. I said pigs."

Ant said, "I am going outside."

"Why, Ant?"

"I don't like the rest of the story.

It has a big bad wolf in it."

I said, "I could change that, Ant.

I could make him a big bad lemon.

Or how about a big bad watermelon?"

"No," said Ant,

"I would know it was a wolf."

Ant went to the door and opened it.

He looked back at me.

He said, "But thank you

for reading to me."

"You are welcome, Ant,"

I said, "anytime."

Ant and the Three Little Figs

Meet the Author

Betsy Byars remembers her father changing certain parts of a story as he read it to her when she was young. This made her look closely at the written word. She always loved books, but she did not start writing books until her children were teenagers. She said, *"In that, writing is like baseball or piano playing. You have got to practice if you want to be successful."*

Meet the Illustrator

Marc Simont was born in Paris, France. Because his parents traveled a lot, he became very skillful at looking closely at the things around him. As a child he taught himself to draw by studying a picture book. He painted portraits and drew illustrations for advertisements before he became an illustrator for children's books. *"I believe that if I like the drawings I do, children will like them also,"* he said.

Theme Connections

Within the Selection

Record your answers to the questions below in the Response Journal section of your Writer's Notebook. In small groups, report the ideas you wrote. Discuss your ideas with the rest of the group. Then choose a person to report your group's answers to the class.

- How did Ant's big brother share the story of "The Three Little Pigs"?
- Why didn't Ant want to hear the rest of the story?

Beyond the Selection

- Have you ever shared a silly story with someone? What was it about?
- Think about what "Ant and the Three Little Figs" tells you about sharing stories.
- Add items to the Concept/Question Board about sharing stories.

Books to the Ceiling

by Arnold Lobel

Books to the ceiling,
   books to the sky.
My piles of books are
   a mile high.
How I love them!
How I need them!
I'll have a long beard by
   the time I read them.

Focus Questions Have you ever shared a story with someone younger? In what ways can books be exciting?

Come Back, Jack!

by Catherine and Laurence Anholt

There was once a little girl who didn't like books. Her mom liked books. Her dad liked books. Her brother, Jack, *loved* books, and he couldn't even read.

"Books are boring," the little girl said. And she went out into the yard to find a real adventure.

"Keep an eye on Jack!" called the little girl's mother as Jack sat down with his book on the grass.

The little girl searched for something
exciting in the garden. She didn't find much.
When she turned around, Jack wasn't
looking at his book . . .

. . . he was crawling *inside* it!

"Come back, Jack!" called the little girl.

But Jack was already gone.

She crawled in after him.

Inside the book was a steep green hill, and at the bottom someone was crying.

"Oh no, he's hurt himself!" said the little girl.

But it wasn't Jack crying at the bottom of the hill. It was Jill.

"Jack fell down—and now he's run away," Jill said.

"Oh dear!" said the little girl. "Come back, Jack!"

The little girl hadn't gone far when she saw
a strange crowd standing outside a house.

"This is the house that Jack built," said a
cow with a crumpled horn.

"Jack isn't old enough to build houses,"
said the little girl. "He can't even read yet."

"But he's a clever lad," said the cow. "Nimble and quick, too. Just watch him jump over that candlestick!"

"Oh dear," said the little girl . . .

"COME BACK, JACK!"

The little girl found herself up in the clouds. She couldn't see Jack. What she could see was a huge castle with its enormous door wide open.

The little girl crept through the castle door—and there was Jack, sitting in a corner, eating a Christmas pie. She was just about to tell him to take out his thumb and eat politely, when the whole castle began to shake.

A great voice roared:

"FEE FI FO FUM,
I'D REALLY LIKE TO
EAT SOMEONE!"

The little girl took hold of Jack's hand, and they ran out of the castle as quickly as they could. But the giant had seen them.

"FUM FO FEE FI, I WANT THOSE CHILDREN IN A PIE!"

Just in time, they found a beanstalk
growing up through the clouds. They started
to climb down it, but the giant was getting
closer. He was about to grab them when . . .

. . . they reached the end of the book and tumbled out into their very own backyard.

The giant's huge, hairy hand stretched out after them, but Jack banged the book shut.

From inside the book came a faraway roar:

"FEE FI FO FUM,
NOW I'VE GONE AND HURT
MY THUMB!"

"Well," said the little girl, "perhaps books aren't boring after all!"

Then she and Jack lay on the grass, and they laughed and laughed and laughed.

Come Back, Jack!

Meet the Author and the Illustrator

Catherine and Laurence Anholt were both born in London, England. They were married in 1984 and soon after began to work together to create their own books. He usually writes the stories and she illustrates them. They want children to see themselves in the stories and to enjoy reading them.

Laurence Anholt first worked as an art teacher and wrote children's books in his free time. Many of his ideas came from listening to his three children talking. *"I want children to get the message that books are fun—it is okay to enjoy yourself."* Catherine Anholt said, *"All my drawings are from memory, although I have always intended to work from life."*

Theme Connections

Within the Selection

Writer's Notebook Record your answers to the questions below in the Response Journal section of your Writer's Notebook. In small groups, report the ideas you wrote. Discuss your ideas with the rest of the group. Then choose a person to report your group's answers to the class.

- How did Jack share stories with his big sister?

- Jack's sister was looking for an adventure outside in the yard. What kind of an adventure did she find instead?

Across Selections

- How are the two main characters in "Come Back, Jack!" and "Ant and the Three Little Figs" alike and different?

Beyond the Selection

- Did anyone show you that books are exciting and interesting? What did that person do to show you that books are fun?

- Think about how "Come Back, Jack!" adds to what you know about sharing stories.

- Add items to the Concept/Question Board about sharing stories.

My Book!

David L. Harrison
illustrated by Anna Rich

I did it!
I did it!
Come and look
At what I've done!
I read a book!
When someone wrote it
Long ago
For me to read,
How did he know
That this was the book
I'd take from the shelf
And lie on the floor
And read by myself?

I really read it!
Just like that!
Word by word,
From first to last!
I'm sleeping with
This book in bed,
This first FIRST book
I've ever read!

THE Library

Sarah Stewart
illustrated by David Small

Elizabeth Brown
Entered the world
Dropping straight down from the sky.

Elizabeth Brown
Entered the world
Skinny, nearsighted, and shy.

47

She didn't like to play with dolls,
She didn't like to skate.
She learned to read quite early
And at an incredible rate.

She always took a book to bed,
With a flashlight under the sheet.
She'd make a tent of covers
And read herself to sleep.

Elizabeth Brown
Went off to school
Dragging a steamer trunk.

Elizabeth Brown
Unpacked her books,
Breaking the upper bunk.

She sat in all her classes
And doodled on a pad,
Adrift in dreams of entering
A readers' olympiad.

She manufactured library cards
And checked out books to friends,
Then shocked them with her midnight raids
To collect the books again.

Elizabeth Brown
Preferred a book
To going on a date.

While friends went out
And danced till dawn,
She stayed up reading late.

51

She took the train one afternoon
And promptly lost her way,
So bought a house and settled down
To tutoring for pay.

Elizabeth Brown
Walked into town
Summer, fall, winter, and spring.

Elizabeth Brown
Walked into town
Looking for only one thing.

She didn't want potato chips,
She didn't want new clothes.
She went straight to the bookstore.
"May I have one of **those**?"

Elizabeth Brown
Walked right back home
And read and read and read.

She even read while
Exercising,
And standing on her head.

54

She made a list of groceries
And tucked it in her book,
Then lost the list among the fruits
And left with nothing to cook.

She read about Greek goddesses
While vacuuming the floor.
Attending only to her book,
She'd walk into a door.

Books were piled on top of chairs
And spread across the floor.
Her shelves began to fall apart,
As she read more and more.

Big books made very solid stacks
On which teacups could rest.
Small books became the building blocks
For busy little guests.

When volumes climbed the parlor walls
And blocked the big front door,
She had to face the awful fact
She could not have one more.

Elizabeth Brown
Walked into town
That very afternoon.

Elizabeth Brown
Walked into town
Whistling a happy tune.

She didn't want a bicycle,
She didn't want silk bows.
She went straight to the courthouse—
"May I have one of **those**?"

The form was for donations.
She quickly wrote this line:
"*I, E. Brown, give to the town
All that was ever mine.*"

Elizabeth Brown
Moved in with a friend
And lived to a ripe old age.

They walked to the library
Day after day,
And turned page . . .
after page . . .

after page.

59

THE Library

Meet the Author

Sarah Stewart grew up in Texas. While growing up she had two favorite places where she loved to go to listen to the silence and explore the world around her. These two places were her grandmother's garden and the library. Stewart spent many days in these places daydreaming and writing. She now lives in a historic home in Michigan with her husband, her dog Simon, and her cat Otis. She also has three children.

Meet the Illustrator

David Small was born in Detroit, Michigan. His father was a doctor— a radiologist. When David Small was a child he learned to draw pictures of people by looking at their x-rays. Looking at people's skeletons taught him why they move and look the way they do. David Small likes to write books too. *"Of all the things I do as an artist, the creation of children's picture books is the most pleasurable,"* he said. David Small feels like he's putting on a whole show when he writes a book and draws the pictures to go with the words.

Theme Connections

Within the Selection

Record your answers to the questions below in the Response Journal section of your Writer's Notebook. In small groups, report the ideas you wrote. Discuss your ideas with the rest of the group. Then choose a person to report your group's answers to the class.

- Why did Elizabeth Brown have so many books?
- How did Elizabeth Brown share her stories with the entire town?

Across Selections

- As a girl, how was Elizabeth Brown different from the girl in "Come Back, Jack!"? How did the girl in "Come Back, Jack!" become more like Elizabeth Brown in the end?

Beyond the Selection

- Think about how "The Library" adds to what you know about sharing stories.
- Add items to the Concept/Question Board about sharing stories.

Story Hour – Starring Megan!

by Julie Brillhart

Once in awhile, when the sitter couldn't come, Megan and her baby brother, Nathan, got to spend an afternoon with their mother at the town library. Their mother was the librarian.

Megan liked the library because she had jobs to do. Her mother called her the "assistant." She put away the children's books and picked up the stuffed animals.

She decorated the bulletin board and watered the plants.

And when things got very, very busy, Megan was always ready to help with Nathan.

But most of all, Megan liked the library because she loved books and was learning to read. She couldn't wait to read every book in the whole library!

Whenever she had a chance, Megan would curl up with *Fly up High* and try to sound out the words. Often she got stuck, and her mother would help her.

Megan would sigh. "Oh, reading is so hard!"

"I know," said her mother. "But keep trying. It will come."

So Megan kept on trying. She tried at
school, in the car, at the supermarket, in the
bathtub, after dinner, and even after lights out!

She had never tried so hard at anything
before.

One time the sitter couldn't come on the day Megan's mother had story hour. "I hope Nathan sleeps through the story," said Megan's mother as the children started to arrive.

Suddenly a stuffed dinosaur came flying through the book slot in the library door. "Oh, good!" said Megan. "Andrew's here!"

Andrew came in carrying a pile of dinosaur books. "Guess what?" said Megan. "I'm learning to read!"

"Oh," said Andrew. "Are there any new books with pteranodons?"

"No," said Megan. "And aren't you ever going to read about *anything* else?"

Megan led the group to the children's room and passed out name tags. She helped the younger children pin on their tags.

"Welcome to story hour," said Megan's mother. "Today I would like to read—"

Right then Nathan let out a howl. Everyone turned to look.

"Just a minute," said Megan's mother. And she got up.

She tried everything to calm Nathan down, but he kept screaming.

The children were getting restless. "Please be patient," said Megan's mother. "I'm sure we will begin shortly."

While all this was going on, Megan sat thinking. Suddenly she had a great idea!

She slipped away and ran to get her favorite book.

Megan sat down in front of all the children. She felt a little scared. "I would like to read *Fly up High*," she said.

Everyone looked at her in amazement. The room became very quiet, and Nathan even stopped crying. Megan began to read.

She read on and on. She showed the
children the pictures, just the way her
mother did. She got stuck on a few words,
but she kept going. Nobody seemed to notice
when she made a mistake.

She read the whole book!

The children all clapped and cheered. And so did some moms and dads who had come in. Megan felt terrific!

She looked over at her mom. "I did it!"
Megan said.

"You sure did," said her mother. "And all by
yourself! I'm very proud of you!"

"I didn't know you could read THAT much," said Andrew. "Can I borrow your book?"

Megan laughed. "Sure," she said. "But it's not about dinosaurs!"

When everyone had gone, Megan's mother gave her a big, big hug. "You were wonderful!" she said. "You saved the day!"

"Yay!" said Megan. "Now I'll read every book in the whole library!"

And she started right away.

Story Hour – Starring Megan!

Meet the Author and Illustrator

Julie Brillhart used to work as a librarian before she began writing and illustrating children's books. Many of the ideas for her books came from working with children in the library. She takes everyday moments and turns them into stories and art.

Although her own children are grown, her favorite thing to do is to go to the children's room at her local library. Every week she spends an afternoon picking out children's books to take home and read.

Theme Connections

Within the Selection

Writer's Notebook

Record your answers to the questions below in the Response Journal section of your Writer's Notebook. In small groups, report the ideas you wrote. Discuss your ideas with the rest of the group. Then choose a person to report your group's answers to the class.

- Megan thought that learning to read was hard. Why did her mother tell her to keep trying?

- How was Megan able to save the day when her mother needed her help?

Across Selections

- How was Megan like Jack in "Come Back, Jack!"?

Beyond the Selection

- Have you ever tried and tried to learn how to do something? How did you feel when you were able to do it?

- Think about how "Story Hour—Starring Megan!" adds to what you know about sharing stories.

- Add items to the Concept/Question Board about sharing stories.

The Library. 1960. **Jacob Lawrence.** Tempera on fiberboard.
60.9 × 75.8 cm. The National Museum of American Art,
Smithsonian Institution, Washington, DC.

Romans Parisiens. **Vincent van Gogh.** Oil on canvas. Private collection.

Jungle Tales. 1895. **James J. Shannon.** Oil on canvas. 87 × 113.7 cm. The Metropolitan Museum of Art.

Tomás and the Library Lady

Pat Mora
illustrated by Raul Colón

It was midnight. The light of the full
moon followed the tired old car. Tomás
was tired too. Hot and tired. He missed his
own bed, in his own house in Texas.

Tomás was on his way to Iowa again with his family. His mother and father were farm workers. They picked fruit and vegetables for Texas farmers in the winter and for Iowa farmers in the summer. Year after year they bump-bumped along in their rusty old car. "Mamá," whispered Tomás, "if I had a glass of cold water, I would drink it in large gulps. I would suck the ice. I would pour the last drops of water on my face."

Tomás was glad when the car finally stopped. He helped his grandfather, Papá Grande, climb down. Tomás said, *"Buenas noches"*—"Good night"—to Papá, Mamá, Papá Grande, and to his little brother, Enrique. He curled up on the cot in the small house that his family shared with the other workers.

Early the next morning Mamá and Papá
went out to pick corn in the green fields. All
day they worked in the hot sun. Tomás and
Enrique carried water to them. Then the
boys played with a ball Mamá had sewn
from an old teddy bear.

When they got hot, they sat under a tree
with Papá Grande. "Tell us the story about
the man in the forest," said Tomás.

Tomás liked to listen to Papá Grande tell
stories in Spanish. Papá Grande was the best
storyteller in the family.

"En un tiempo pasado," Papá Grande began. "Once upon a time . . . on a windy night a man was riding a horse through a forest. The wind was howling, *whooooooooo,* and the leaves were blowing, *whish, whish . . .*

"All of a sudden something grabbed the man. He couldn't move. He was too scared to look around. All night long he wanted to ride away. But he couldn't.

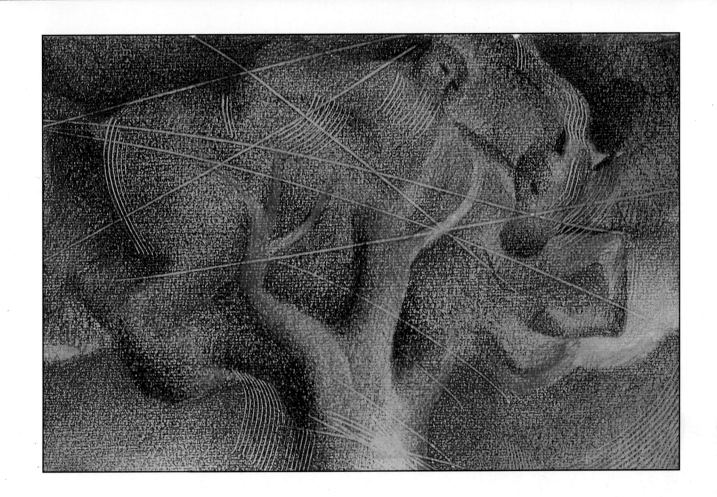

"How the wind howled, *whoooooooooo*. How the leaves blew. How his teeth chattered!

"Finally the sun came up. Slowly the man turned around. And who do you think was holding him?"

Tomás smiled and said, "A thorny tree."

Papá Grande laughed. "Tomás, you know all my stories," he said. "There are many more in the library. You are big enough to go by yourself. Then you can teach us new stories."

The next morning Tomás walked downtown. He looked at the big library. Its tall windows were like eyes glaring at him. Tomás walked around and around the big building. He saw children coming out carrying books. Slowly he started climbing up, up the steps. He counted them to himself in Spanish. *Uno, dos, tres, cuatro* . . . His mouth felt full of cotton.

Tomás stood in front of the library doors. He pressed his nose against the glass and peeked in. The library was huge!

A hand tapped his shoulder. Tomás jumped.
A tall lady looked down at him. "It's a hot
day," she said. "Come inside and have a drink
of water. What's your name?" she asked.

"Tomás," he said.

"Come, Tomás," she said.

Inside it was cool. Tomás had never seen so many books. The lady watched him. "Come," she said again, leading him to a drinking fountain. "First some water. Then I will bring books to this table for you. What would you like to read about?"

"Tigers. Dinosaurs," said Tomás.

Tomás drank the cold water. He looked at the tall ceiling. He looked at all the books around the room. He watched the lady take some books from the shelves and bring them to the table. "This chair is for you, Tomás," she said. Tomás sat down. Then very carefully he took a book from the pile and opened it.

Tomás saw dinosaurs bending their long necks to lap shiny water. He heard the cries of a wild snakebird. He felt the warm neck of the dinosaur as he held on tight for a ride. Tomás forgot about the library lady. He forgot about Iowa and Texas.

"Tomás, Tomás," said the library lady softly. Tomás looked around. The library was empty. The sun was setting.

The library lady looked at Tomás for a long time. She said, "Tomás, would you like to borrow two library books? I will check them out in my name."

Tomás walked out of the library carrying his books. He ran home, eager to show the new stories to his family.

Papá Grande looked at the library books. "Read to me," he said to Tomás. First Tomás showed him the pictures. He pointed to the tiger. *"¡Qué tigre tan grande!"* Tomás said first in Spanish and then in English, "What a big tiger!"

"Read to me in English," said Papá Grande. Tomás read about tiger eyes shining brightly in the jungle at night. He roared like a huge tiger. Papá, Mamá, and Enrique laughed. They came and sat near him to hear his story.

Some days Tomás went with his parents to the town dump. They looked for pieces of iron to sell. Enrique looked for toys. Tomás looked for books. He would put the books in the sun to bake away the smell.

All summer, whenever he could, Tomás went to the library. The library lady would say, "First a drink of water and then some new books, Tomás."

On quiet days the library lady said, "Come to my desk and read to me, Tomás." Then she would say, "Please teach me some new words in Spanish."

Tomás would smile. He liked being the teacher. The library lady pointed to a book. "Book is *libro*," said Tomás.

"*Libro*," said the library lady.

"*Pájaro*," said Tomás, flapping his arms.

The library lady laughed. "Bird," she said.

On days when the library was busy, Tomás read to himself. He'd look at the pictures for a long time. He smelled the smoke at an Indian camp. He rode a black horse across a hot, dusty desert.

And in the evenings he would read the stories to Mamá, Papá, Papá Grande, and Enrique.

One August afternoon Tomás brought Papá Grande to the library.

The library lady said, "*Buenas tardes, señor.*" Tomás smiled. He had taught the library lady how to say "Good afternoon, sir" in Spanish.

"*Buenas tardes, señora,*" Papá Grande replied.

Softly Tomás said, "I have a sad word to teach you today. The word is *adiós*. It means good-bye."

Tomás was going back to Texas. He would miss this quiet place, the cool water, the many books. He would miss the library lady.

"My mother sent this to thank you," said Tomás, handing her a small package. "It is *pan dulce*, sweet bread. My mother makes the best *pan dulce* in Texas."

The library lady said, "How nice. How very nice. *Gracias*, Tomás. Thank you." She gave Tomás a big hug.

That night, bumping along again in the tired old car, Tomás held a shiny new book, a present from the library lady. Papá Grande smiled and said, "More stories for the new storyteller."

Tomás closed his eyes. He saw the
dinosaurs drinking cool water long ago. He
heard the cry of the wild snakebird. He felt
the warm neck of the dinosaur as he held on
tight for a bumpy ride.

Tomás and the Library Lady

Meet the Author

Pat Mora's family spoke two languages at home, so she learned to speak and write in both English and Spanish. She was able to use both in her writing, as in "Tomás and the Library Lady." Pat Mora was a teacher for nearly twenty years before she began a career as a writer. She writes poetry and nonfiction, as well as children's literature. *"I've always enjoyed reading all kinds of books and now I get to write them too, to sit and play with words on my computer."*

Meet the Illustrator

Raul Colón dreamed of becoming an artist as a young child. He would hand in his homework with doodles and drawings. He likes to scratch the paper with a special tool before he uses colored pencils. This gives his illustrations a special effect. His work has included puppet designs, album covers, short animated films, and illustrations for children's books.

Theme Connections

Within the Selection

Record your answers to the questions below in the Response Journal section of your Writer's Notebook. In small groups, report the ideas you wrote. Discuss your ideas with the rest of the group. Then choose a person to report your group's answers to the class.

- Why did Tomás decide to go to the library?
- What talent did Tomás and his grandfather share?

Across Selections

- What other stories have you read about sharing stories?
- What do Jack, Megan, Elizabeth Brown, and Tomás have in common?

Beyond the Selection

- Does your family ever tell or read stories to each other? What types of stories do they tell or read?
- Think about how "Tomás and the Library Lady" adds to what you know about sharing stories.
- Add items to the Concept/Question Board about sharing stories.

W hat does it mean to be kind? Who is kind? How do you know? Stories can help us learn about kindness.

Mushroom in the Rain

retold by Mirra Ginsburg
illustrated by José Aruego and Ariane Dewey

One day an ant was caught in the rain.
"Where can I hide?" he wondered.
   He saw a tiny mushroom peeking out of
the ground in a clearing, and he hid under it.
He sat there, waiting for the rain to stop. But
the rain came down harder and harder.

A wet butterfly crawled up to the mushroom.

"Cousin Ant, let me come in from the rain. I am so wet I cannot fly."

"How can I let you in?" said the ant. "There is barely room enough for one."

"It does not matter," said the butterfly. "Better crowded than wet."

The ant moved over and made room for the butterfly. The rain came down harder and harder.

A mouse ran up.

"Let me in under the mushroom. I am drenched to the bone."

"How can we let you in? There is no more room here."

"Just move a little closer!"

They huddled closer and let the mouse in. And the rain came down and came down and would not stop.

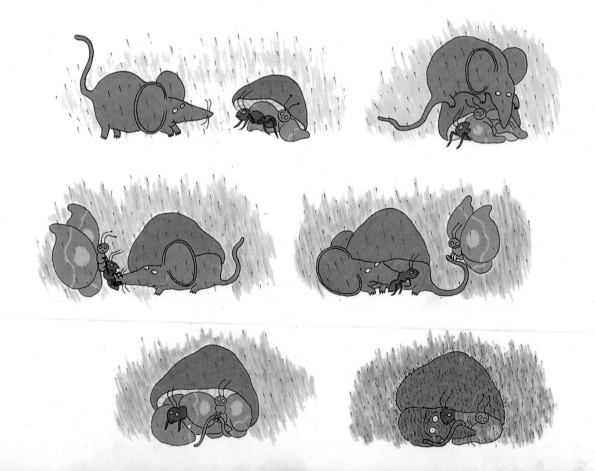

A little sparrow hopped up to the mushroom, crying: "My feathers are dripping, my wings are so tired! Let me in under the mushroom to dry out and rest until the rain stops!"

"But there is no room here."

"Please! Move over just a little!"

They moved over, and there was room enough for the sparrow.

Then a rabbit hopped into the clearing and saw the mushroom.

"Oh, hide me!" he cried. "Save me! A fox is chasing me!"

"Poor rabbit," said the ant. "Let's crowd ourselves a little more and take him in."

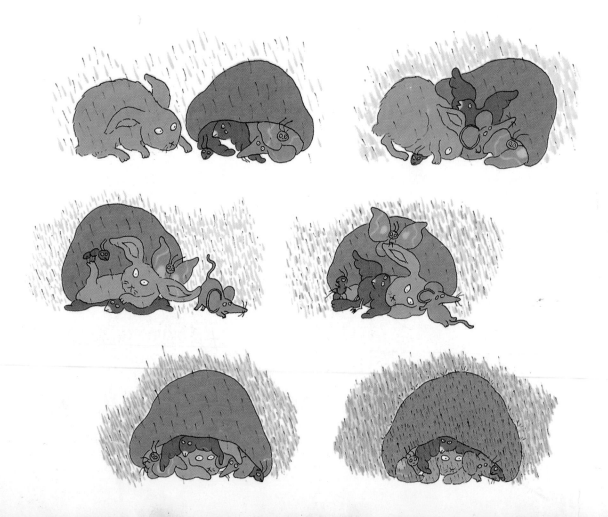

As soon as they hid the rabbit, the fox
came running.

"Have you seen the rabbit? Which way did
he go?" he asked.

"We have not seen him."

The fox came nearer and sniffed. "There is
a rabbit smell around. Isn't he hiding here?"

"You silly fox! How could a rabbit get in here? Don't you see there isn't any room?"

The fox turned up his nose, flicked his tail, and ran off.

By then the rain was over. The sun looked out from behind the clouds. And everyone came out from under the mushroom, bright and merry.

The ant looked at his neighbors. "How could this be? At first I had hardly room enough under the mushroom just for myself, and in the end all five of us were able to sit under it."

"Qua-ha-ha! Qua-ha-ha!" somebody laughed loudly behind them.

They turned and saw a fat green frog sitting on top of the mushroom, shaking his head at them.

"Qua-ha-ha!" said the frog. "Don't you know what happens to a mushroom in the rain?" And he hopped away, still laughing.

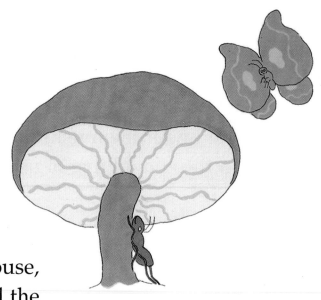

The ant, the
butterfly, the mouse,
the sparrow, and the
rabbit looked at one another, then at the
mushroom. And suddenly they knew why
there was room enough under the mushroom
for them all.

Do you know? Can you guess what
happens to a mushroom when it rains?

IT GROWS!

Mushroom in the Rain

Meet the Author

Mirra Ginsburg was born in a small Russian village much like the towns in the folktales that she loved to read. She began writing children's books by taking books written in Russian or Yiddish and rewriting them in English so that American children could enjoy them. Before long, she was making up her own stories. She said, *"From my father, I learned to love animals and green growing things. As a child, I was surrounded with them."*

Meet the Illustrators

José Aruego and Ariane Dewey have combined their talents and have illustrated more than sixty children's books. Mr. Aruego does the drawings and Ms. Dewey adds the color through paint. José Aruego began a career in law, but after a few months he realized that he wanted to draw, not practice law. After graduating from art school, he began drawing cartoons and later began illustrating children's books. Ariane Dewey always loved bright colors. In fourth grade art class, she painted bright pink kids swimming in a blue-green lake. Her love of joyful colors is seen in many children's books.

118

Theme Connections

Within the Selection

Record your answers to the questions below in the Response Journal section of your Writer's Notebook. In small groups, report the ideas you wrote. Discuss your ideas with the rest of the group. Then choose a person to report your group's answers to the class.

- How could the mushroom give shelter to all the animals?
- Why were the animals kind to the rabbit? Why were the animals not kind to the fox?

Across Selections

- Compare how the ant in this story and Amber in "Amber on the Mountain" showed kindness by sharing.

Beyond the Selection

- Think about what "A Mushroom in the Rain" tells you about kindness.
- Add items to the Concept/Question Board about kindness.

The Elves and the Shoemaker

retold by Freya Littledale
illustrated by Brinton Turkle

There was once a good shoemaker who became very poor. At last he had only one piece of leather to make one pair of shoes. "Well," said the shoemaker to his wife, "I will cut the leather tonight and make the shoes in the morning."

The next morning he went to his table, and he couldn't believe what he saw. The leather was polished. The sewing was done. And there was a fine pair of shoes! Not one stitch was out of place.

"Do you see what I see?" asked the shoemaker.

"Indeed I do," said his wife. "I see a fine pair of shoes."

"But who could have made them?" the shoemaker said.

"It's just like magic!" said his wife.

At that very moment a man came in with a top hat and cane. "Those shoes look right for me," said the man. And so they were. They were right from heel to toe. "How much do they cost?"

"One gold coin," said the shoemaker.

"I'll give you two," said the man.

And he went on his way with a smile on his face and the new shoes on his feet.

"Well, well," said the shoemaker, "now I can buy leather for two pairs of shoes." And he cut the leather that night so he could make the shoes in the morning.

The next morning the shoemaker woke up, and he found two pairs of ladies' shoes. They were shining in the sunlight.

"Who is making these shoes?" said the shoemaker. "They are the best shoes in the world."

At that very moment two ladies came in.
They looked exactly alike. "My, what pretty
shoes!" said the ladies. "They will surely fit
us." And the ladies were right. They gave the
shoemaker four gold coins and away they
went . . . clickety-clack, clickety-clack in
their pretty new shoes.

Fine Shoemaking

And so it went. Every night the shoemaker cut the leather. Every morning the shoes were made. And every day more people came to buy his beautiful shoes.

Just before Christmas the shoemaker said, "Whoever is making these shoes is making us very happy."

"And rich," said his wife.

"Let us stay up and see who it is," the shoemaker said.

"Good," said his wife. So they hid behind some coats, and they waited and waited and waited. When the clock struck twelve, in came two little elves.

"*Elves*," cried the shoemaker.

"Shh!" said his wife.

At once the elves hopped up on the table and set to work. Tap-tap went their hammers. Snip-snap went their scissors. Stitch-stitch went their needles. Their tiny fingers moved so fast the shoemaker and his wife could hardly believe their eyes.

The elves sewed and they hammered and they didn't stop until all the shoes were finished. There were little shoes and big ones. There were white ones and black ones and brown ones. The elves lined them all in a row. Then they jumped down from the table. They ran across the room and out the door.

The next morning the wife said, "The elves have made us very happy. I want to make them happy too. They need new clothes to keep warm. So I'll make them pants and shirts and coats. And I'll knit them socks and hats. You can make them each a pair of shoes."

"Yes, yes!" said the shoemaker. And they went right to work.

On Christmas Eve the shoemaker left no leather on the table. He left all the pretty gifts instead. Then he and his wife hid behind the coats to see what the elves would do.

When the clock struck twelve, in came the elves, ready to set to work. But when they looked at the table and saw the fine clothes, they laughed and clapped their hands.

"How happy they are!" said the shoemaker's wife.

"Shhh," said her husband.

133

The elves put on the clothes, looked in the mirror, and began to sing:

What fine and handsome elves are we,
No longer cobblers will we be,
From now on we'll dance and play,
Into the woods and far away.

They hopped over the table and jumped over the chairs. They skipped all around the room, danced out the door, and were never seen again. But from that night on everything always went well for the good shoemaker and his wife.

The Elves and the Shoemaker

Meet the Author

Freya Littledale spent much of her free time as a child reading. She especially enjoyed fairy tales. When she was nine-years old, she began writing her own stories and poems. She always loved writing and retelling stories for children. Littledale kept sharing her stories for the rest of her life.

Meet the Illustrator

Brinton Turkle has added his special magic to more than fifty children's books. *"I find the combination of words and pictures that is possible today only in children's books very exciting . . . children [who] must never be offered less than the very best."*

Theme Connections

Within the Selection

Writer's Notebook Record your answers to the questions below in the Response Journal section of your Writer's Notebook. In small groups, report the ideas you wrote. Discuss your ideas with the rest of the group. Then choose a person to report your group's answers to the class.

- How did the poor shoemaker and his wife become rich and successful?
- Do you think the elves expected the shoemaker to return their kindness? Why or why not?

Across Selections

- What rewards did the different characters in this story and in "Mushroom in the Rain" receive for their kindness?

Beyond the Selection

- Have you ever returned kindness to someone who was kind to you? What did you do?
- Think about how "The Elves and the Shoemaker" adds to what you know about kindness.
- Add items to the Concept/Question Board about kindness.

The Paper Crane

by Molly Bang

A man once owned a restaurant on a
busy road. He loved to cook good
food and he loved to serve it. He
worked from morning until night, and he
was happy.

138

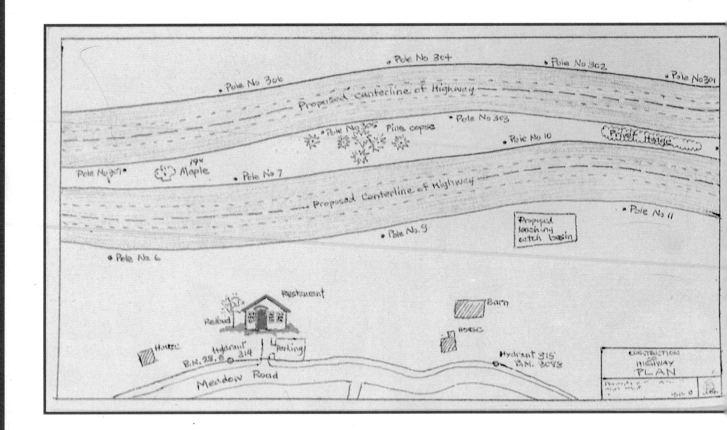

But a new highway was built close by. Travelers drove straight from one place to another and no longer stopped at the restaurant. Many days went by when no guests came at all. The man became very poor, and had nothing to do but dust and polish his empty plates and tables.

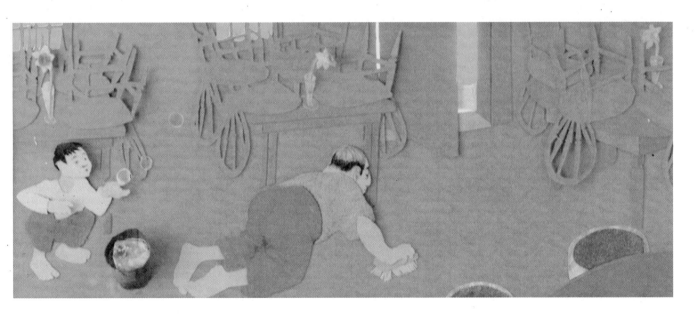

One evening a stranger came into the restaurant. His clothes were old and worn, but he had an unusual, gentle manner.

Though he said he had no money to pay
for food, the owner invited him to sit down.
He cooked the best meal he could make and
served him like a king.

When the stranger had finished, he said to his host, "I cannot pay you with money, but I would like to thank you in my own way."

He picked up a paper napkin from the table and folded it into the shape of a crane. "You have only to clap your hands," he said, "and this bird will come to life and dance for you. Take it, and enjoy it while it is with you."

With these words the stranger left.

145

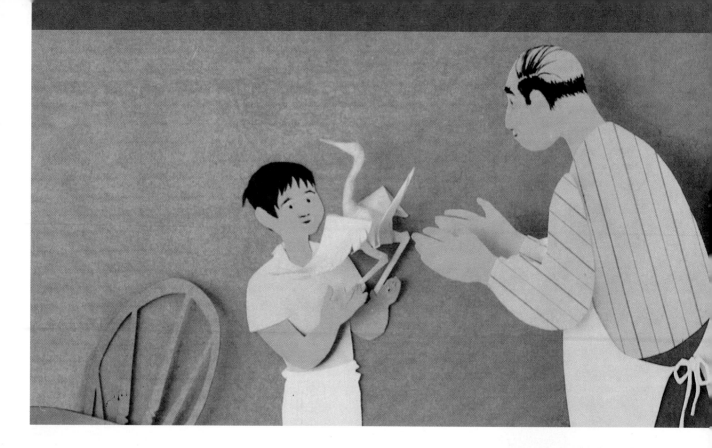

It happened just as the stranger had said.
The owner had only to clap his hands and
the paper crane became a living bird, flew
down to the floor, and danced.

146

Soon word of the dancing crane spread,
and people came from far and near to see the
magic bird perform.

The owner was happy again, for his
restaurant was always full of guests.

He cooked and served and had company
from morning until night.

The weeks passed.

And the months.

One evening a man came into the
restaurant. His clothes were old and worn,
but he had an unusual, gentle manner. The
owner knew him at once and was overjoyed.

The stranger, however, said nothing. He took a flute from his pocket, raised it to his lips, and began to play.

The crane flew down from its place on the shelf and danced as it had never danced before.

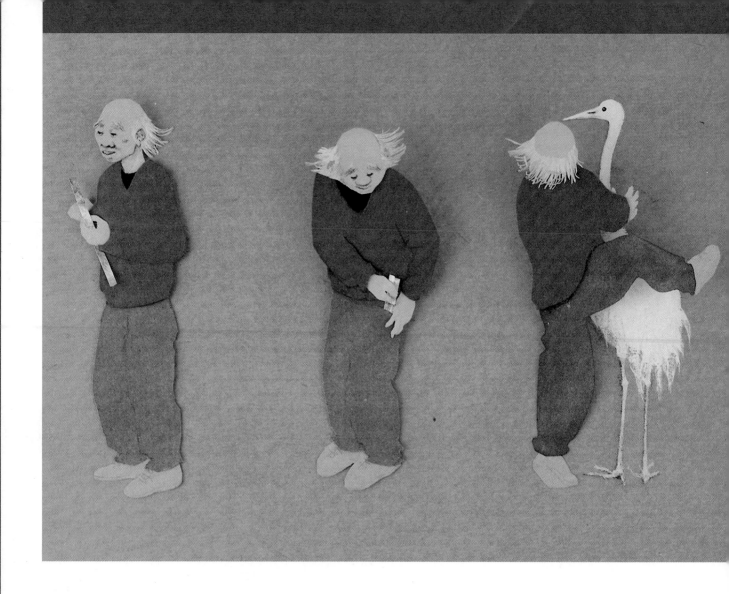

The stranger finished playing, lowered the flute from his lips, and returned it to his pocket. He climbed on the back of the crane, and they flew out of the door and away.

The restaurant still stands by the side of the road, and guests still come to eat the good food and hear the story of the gentle stranger and the magic crane made from a paper napkin. But neither the stranger nor the dancing crane has ever been seen again.

The Paper Crane

Meet the Author and Illustrator

Molly Bang's love of books began early. Her parents often gave each other books for birthdays and other holidays. After graduating from Wellesley College, she went to Japan to teach English.

Through her travels in other countries she has gathered many ideas for her books. In her writings she likes to blend Asian folktale themes with modern settings. Her illustrations show a real understanding of the people and places she writes about. She has even illustrated books for her mother, who is also an author.

Theme Connections

Within the Selection

Writer's Notebook Record your answers to the questions below in the Response Journal section of your Writer's Notebook. In small groups, report the ideas you wrote. Discuss your ideas with the rest of the group. Then choose a person to report your group's answers to the class.

- Why do you think the stranger gave the restaurant owner the paper crane?
- How was the paper crane able to help the restaurant owner?

Across Selections

- What are some ways that "The Paper Crane" and "The Elves and the Shoemaker" are alike?

Beyond the Selection

- Think about how "The Paper Crane" adds to what you know about kindness.
- Add items to the Concept/Question Board about kindness.

Butterfly House

by Eve Bunting

illustrated by Greg Shed

When I was just a little girl
I saw a small black creature
like a tiny worm,
and saved it from a greedy jay
who wanted it
for lunch.

I carried it inside,
safe on its wide green leaf.
My grandpa said
it was a larva
and soon would be
a butterfly.

156

157

We laid the larva carefully
on thistle leaves
inside an empty jar,
put in a twig
for it to climb—
then made a lid
of soft white paper
all stuck around with glue.
My grandpa knew
exactly what to do.
"I raised a butterfly myself," he said,
"when I was just your age."

How strange to think
my grandpa once
was young like me.
"We would have been best friends
if I'd been there back then," I said.
My grandpa smiled.
"It worked out anyhow.
We're best friends now."

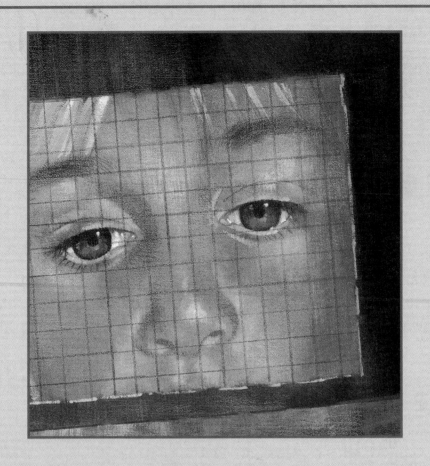

Up in his room
we found a box.
I cut a window in its side,
then covered it with screen.
Soon I could look inside and see
my larva
looking back at me.

What would she see?
A human face
so big and scary,
strange and starey?
What would she think?

160

"I want it pretty till she goes," I said.
And so
Grandpa and I drew flowers
on colored paper.
Cone flowers, purple-blue,
and marigolds,
lantana, bright as flame,
and thistles, too.

We wedged a garden twig inside the box
for her to walk on,
so her wings could dry
once she became a butterfly.

My grandpa knows
the flowers
butterflies like best.
The ones where they can rest
and drink
the sweet, clear nectar.

We glued the painted flowers inside the box
so it was bright with color.
Made a sky above
the lid all blue
with small white cotton clouds,
and green with tops of trees
that seemed to sway
in soundless air.

I made a curve of rainbow
like a hug
to keep her safe
while she was there.
We set the jar inside and closed the painted lid.
Through the screened window
I could see the garden house.
A place of flowers
and space
and waiting stillness.

Each day I put out leaves for food
and watched my larva change.

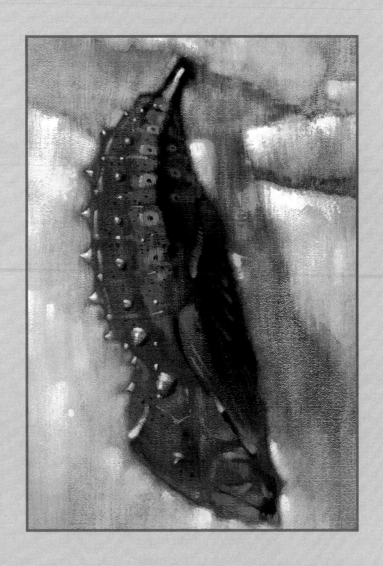

My Grandpa knew when it was time
to gently pull away
the paper top she hung from.
I taped it to the wall inside her house
and let her be.
She would hang free
inside the chrysalis
that kept her hidden from the world.

Inside that magic place
she grew,
transformed herself,
came out, drooped, limp and slack,
with crumpled wings.
She was a butterfly,
all spotted, orange, black, and brown
as if someone had shaken paints
and let the drops fall down.

165

"Our Painted Lady," Grandpa said.
"It's time."
  He meant that it was time
  for her to leave
  for her new life.
  I swallowed tears.
  From the beginning I had known
  today would come.
  Now it was here.
  My grandpa took my hand.
"Cry if you like," he said.
"We understand."

We carried out the box and raised the lid.
I watched her falter
as she felt
the first warm touch of sun,
saw trees,
felt breezes brush across her wings.
She rose,
then rested on the fig tree branch.
I saw her fly.

"Good-bye."

169

So many years have passed.

I am as old as Grandpa was
that spring when I was young.
I live in the house
that once was his.

The garden glows
with cone flowers, purple-blue,
and marigolds,
lantana, bright as flame.
And thistles, too.

Now every spring
the Painted Ladies come.
They float and drift like blossoms.
When I walk
they flutter by
to kiss me
with a painted wing.
Sometimes they cling
as though I am a flower myself.

My neighbors cannot understand.
"Our flowers are the same as yours,"
  they say each time they visit me.
"We even planted thistles
  to invite the butterflies,
  but they don't come.
They fill your air
  like autumn leaves
  although it isn't fall.
It's such a mystery."

I smile.
It's not a mystery at all.

I think my Painted Ladies
talk among themselves
of how their great-great-grandma,
too far back to say,
was saved
from being eaten by a jay.

"This young girl made a house for her,"
they whisper as they fly.
"A painted garden in a box,
so she'd see beauty
as she hung in that half sleep
that we've all known."

"This is the girl,
   but older now.
   We visit her each spring
   to give her back
   the love she gave to us
   so long ago."

It's not a mystery to me.
I think I know.

Butterfly House

Meet the Author

Eve Bunting grew up in Ireland. Nine years after she got married, she and her family moved to the United States. Eve Bunting's children had never heard about Halloween until they came to America. They loved trick-or-treat, and Halloween became their favorite holiday. Many of Eve Bunting's books are about ghosts. She believes the world is full of ideas for her stories. *"I couldn't possibly write about all the interesting things I see. There aren't enough hours in the day,"* she said. Bunting has used her ideas to write about horses running free, kings, sharks, whales, and many other things.

Meet the Illustrator

Greg Shed began attending drawing classes right after high school. He was influenced by the impressionists and, with a lot of practice, taught himself how to paint. Shed began illustrating books when his family and friends encouraged him to share his work with publishers. Shed enjoys combining his artistic talents and passion for American history in children's books. He enjoys music, traveling, and ancient cultures.

Theme Connections

Within the Selection

Writer's Notebook Record your answers to the questions below in the Response Journal section of your Writer's Notebook. In small groups, report the ideas you wrote. Discuss your ideas with the rest of the group. Then choose a person to report your group's answers to the class.

- How did the little girl show kindness to the larva?
- How did the grandfather show kindness?
- Why do the butterflies return each spring?

Across Selections

- How is the kindness in this story like the kindness in "Mushroom in the Rain"?
- What other stories have you read that are about showing kindness to animals?

Beyond the Selection

- Think about what "Butterfly House" tells you about kindness.
- Add items to the Concept/Question Board about kindness.

The Good Samaritan. 1618–1622. **Domenico Fetti.** Oil on wood. 60 × 43.2 cm. The Metropolitan Museum of Art, New York, NY.

General and Horse from the Tomb of Emperor Tang Taizong. 7th century. Stone relief. University of Pennsylvania Museum.

Susan Comforting the Baby. 1881. **Mary Cassatt.** Oil on canvas. The Museum of Fine Arts, Houston.

Corduroy

by Don Freeman

Corduroy is a bear who once lived in
the toy department of a big store.
Day after day he waited with all the
other animals and dolls for someone to
come along and take him home.

The store was always filled with shoppers
buying all sorts of things, but no one ever
seemed to want a small bear in green
overalls.

180

Then one morning a little girl stopped and looked straight into Corduroy's bright eyes.

"Oh, Mommy!" she said. "Look! There's the very bear I've always wanted."

"Not today, dear." Her mother sighed. "I've spent too much already. Besides, he doesn't look new. He's lost the button to one of his shoulder straps."

Corduroy watched them sadly as they walked away.

"I didn't know I'd lost a button," he said to himself. "Tonight I'll go and see if I can find it."

Late that evening, when all the shoppers had gone and the doors were shut and locked, Corduroy climbed carefully down from his shelf and began searching everywhere on the floor for his lost button.

Suddenly he felt the floor moving under him! Quite by accident he had stepped onto an escalator—and up he went!

"Could this be a mountain?" he wondered. "I think I've always wanted to climb a mountain."

He stepped off the escalator as it
reached the next floor, and there, before
his eyes, was a most amazing sight—
tables and chairs and lamps and sofas, and
rows and rows of beds. "This must be a
palace!" Corduroy gasped. "I guess I've
always wanted to live in a palace."

He wandered around admiring the
furniture.

"This must be a bed," he said. "I've
always wanted to sleep in a bed." And up
he crawled onto a large, thick mattress.

All at once he saw something small
and round.

"Why, here's my button!" he cried.
And he tried to pick it up. But, like all the
other buttons on the mattress, it was tied
down tight.

He yanked and pulled with both paws
until POP! Off came the button—and off
the mattress Corduroy toppled, *bang* into a
tall floor lamp. Over it fell with a crash!

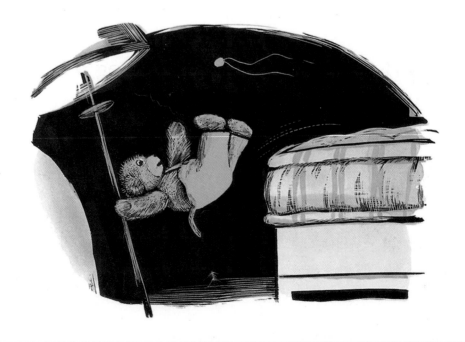

Corduroy didn't know it, but there was someone else awake in the store. The night watchman was going his rounds on the floor above. When he heard the crash he came dashing down the escalator.

"Now who in the world did that!" he exclaimed. "Somebody must be hiding around here!"

He flashed his light under and over sofas and beds until he came to the biggest bed of all. And there he saw two fuzzy brown ears sticking up from under the cover.

"Hello!" he said. "How did *you* get upstairs?"

The watchman tucked Corduroy under
his arm and carried him down the
escalator and set him on the shelf in the
toy department with the other animals
and dolls.

Corduroy was just waking up when the first customers came into the store in the morning. And there, looking at him with a wide, warm smile, was the same little girl he'd seen only the day before.

"I'm Lisa," she said, "and you're going to be my very own bear. Last night I counted what I've saved in my piggy bank and my mother said I could bring you home."

"Shall I put him in a box for you?" the saleslady asked.

"Oh, no thank you," Lisa answered. And she carried Corduroy home in her arms.

She ran all the way up four flights of stairs, into her family's apartment, and straight to her own room.

Corduroy blinked. There was a chair and a chest of drawers, and alongside a girl-size bed stood a little bed just the right size for him. The room was small, nothing like that enormous palace in the department store.

"This must be home," he said. "I *know* I've always wanted a home!"

Lisa sat down with Corduroy on her lap
and began to sew a button on his overalls.
"I like you the way you are," she said,
"but you'll be more comfortable with your
shoulder strap fastened."

"You must be a friend," said Corduroy.
"I've always wanted a friend."
"Me too!" said Lisa, and gave him a
big hug.

Corduroy

Meet the Author and Illustrator

Don Freeman had a job playing the trumpet until he left his trumpet in the subway in New York City. He forgot his trumpet because he was so busy drawing for his art class. From then on, Freeman made his living drawing pictures. Freeman wrote and illustrated his first children's book for his young son, Roy. Many more books followed, including "Corduroy."

Theme Connections

Within the Selection

Record your answers to the questions below in the Response Journal section of your Writer's Notebook. In small groups, report the ideas you wrote. Discuss your ideas with the rest of the group. Then choose a person to report your group's answers to the class.

- How was Lisa kind to Corduroy?
- Who else in the story was kind to Corduroy? What did he do?

Across Selections

- How was Lisa's kindness to Corduroy similar to the kindness the restaurant owner showed to the stranger?

Beyond the Selection

- Would you choose a bear like Corduroy if you saw him in a store? Why or why not?
- Think about how "Corduroy" adds to what you know about kindness.
- Add items to the Concept/Question Board about kindness.

April Medicine

Joyce Carol Thomas
illustrated by Floyd Cooper

My mother's touch, so tender, so certain
Steadies me with healing hands
Hands that cool my brow when I perspire
And warm me when I shiver

My mother's hands already know
The temperature of my head
The weather of my heart
How do they know to be cool when I'm hot
And warm when I'm not?

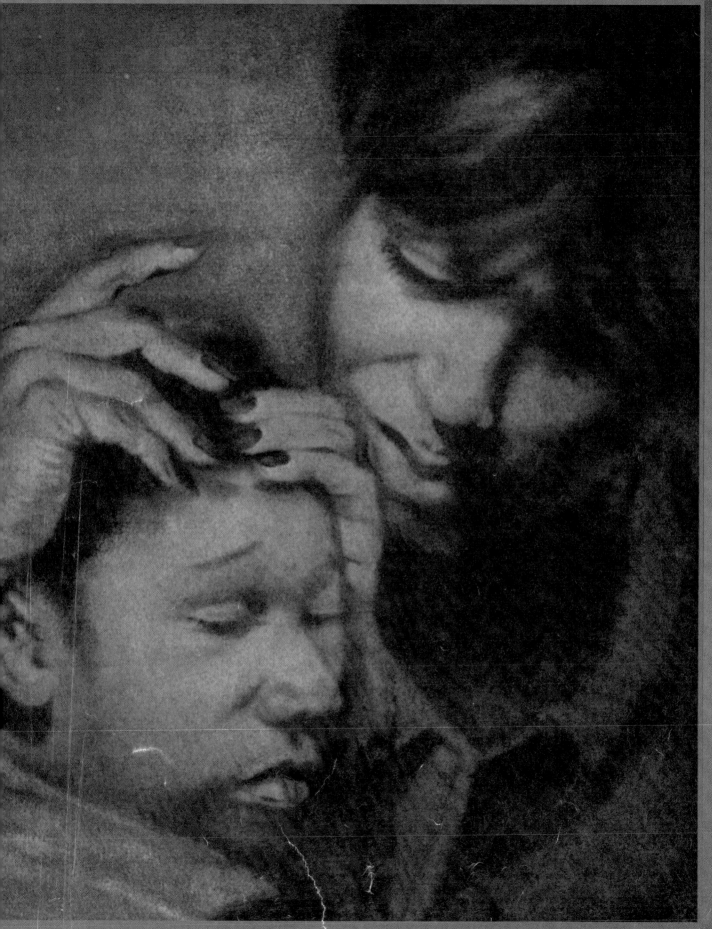

Focus Questions How can kindness spread to others?
Can kindness be a team effort?

The Story of Three Whales

Giles Whittell
illustrated by Patrick Benson

For twelve bright weeks every summer,
the Arctic Ocean is full of life. Blooms of
plankton float among the icebergs. Shellfish
slide along the sea floor. Squid lurk under
pitch-black overhangs of rock. And whales
swim up from the Pacific to feed.

Humpback whales, Bowhead whales and California Gray whales all come to the Arctic. In the summer of 1988 one particular herd of California Grays was plunging and rolling, leaping and belly-flopping, off the north coast of Alaska.

But winter came early in 1988. The first sign was a freezing wind from the east. Blizzards blew in from the top of the world. Thick pack-ice spread out from the shore and its shadow fell over the whales.

Most of the whales were quick to sense the changes. In small groups, they set off on the long swim south to warmth for the winter. But three of the whales failed to notice the end of summer—one adult, one middle-sized, one baby.

Quietly the ice crept in. The ocean was changing from blue to silent white. Gray whales hold their breath under water for half an hour, but soon the three who had been left behind would have nowhere left to surface.

Only the open water was safe, beyond the pack-ice. But the three whales lost their sense of direction. They swam toward land, into an Alaskan bay, where the still, shallow water was certain to freeze very quickly.

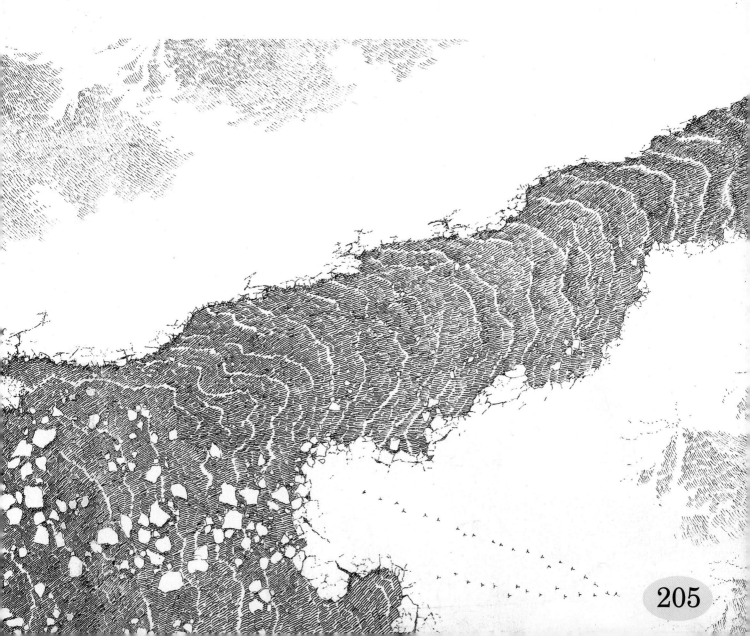

At the mouth of the bay was a shelf of ice, under water. Broken pack-ice piled up against it, forming a wall. From sea-bed to surface there was no way out.

Then the surface froze solid. The whales were trapped in a prison of ice. They could not breathe. Again and again they rammed upward at the ice with their noses.

At last they managed to push their great heads through a crack in the ice. An Inuit hunter was passing and saw them. In nearby Barrow, an Inuit town, he told people what he had seen.

To begin with nothing was done to save the whales. It would be natural for the whales to die and the Inuit accepted it. But the news of the whales began to spread. Their pictures appeared on local TV.

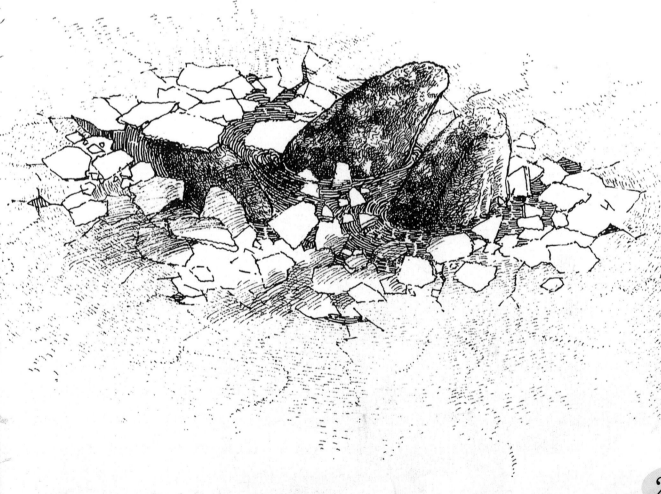

One person who heard the news was
a wildlife ranger. She persuaded the
people of Barrow to help keep the whales
alive. Out over the ice they trudged, with
axes, ice-poles and chainsaws to cut
breathing holes.

The whales appeared at the holes and
filled their huge lungs. The Inuit gave them
names: Siku (the biggest), Poutu (the middle
one) and Kannick (the baby). *Siku* means
ice in Inuit. *Poutu* means ice-hole and
Kannick means snowflake.

The Inuit cut a line of breathing holes, out toward the open water. They worked for fourteen days and nights. Clattering chainsaws sliced constantly through the ice, but the water would quickly freeze solid again.

Siku, Poutu and Kannick refused to follow the line of holes. They stayed by the shore where they knew they could breathe. "The Plight of the Whales" became front-page news all over the world. Millions of people waited in hope.

From all across America, offers of help poured in. But nothing could break through the wall of ice at the mouth of the bay. An enormous bulldozer tried, but stuck fast.

A sky-crane helicopter hammered the ice
with a concrete torpedo. It punched a line
of holes from the whales to the wall. But
still the whales wouldn't follow.

Their noses were bloody and scraped to the bone. The ice was invincible. It seemed to the watching world that the whales must die. Polar bears stalked the ice, waiting patiently for a feast of whale-meat.

One evening Siku and Poutu surfaced alone. Being the smallest, Kannick was also the weakest. Morning came and still only Siku and Poutu appeared at the hole. No one could say exactly what had happened. And no one ever saw Kannick again.

On the twentieth day, Siku and Poutu felt the tremble of distant engines. A huge Russian ice-breaker was roaring to the rescue, the great *Admiral Makarov*.

The captain found a grand phrase to mark the occasion. "Let us begin to break ice!" he called. All night the breaker charged at the ice, pulled back, and charged again.

By morning a channel was clear, a quarter of a mile wide. The crew of the *Admiral Makarov* grinned. They came ashore to celebrate and the Inuit and other Americans hugged them and cheered.

Then the ice-breaker turned for the open sea with Siku and Poutu close behind. The whales understood that they must follow the thunder and froth of the engines. The sound would lead them from the prison of ice, to the open water and freedom.

The rest of the herd was three weeks ahead on the journey south. Siku and Poutu had thousands of miles to swim. So they each blew a great waterspout and set off.

Their long ordeal was over now.

The Story of Three Whales

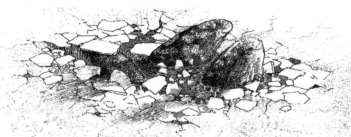

Meet the Author

Giles Whittell grew up in Kenya, Nigeria, and Algeria. In 1989 he rode his bicycle from Berlin to Bulgaria and then wrote about his trip. He is a reporter for a newspaper in Los Angeles.

Meet the Illustrator

Patrick Benson was born and lives in England. He worked in filmmaking and sculpture before he began illustrating books for children. He has illustrated twenty-five children's books. *"What I really want is to get good pictures to as many children as possible."*

220

Theme Connections

Within the Selection

Writer's Notebook Record your answers to the questions below in the Response Journal section of your Writer's Notebook. In small groups, report the ideas you wrote. Discuss your ideas with the rest of the group. Then choose a person to report your group's answers to the class.

- Why did the people care about the whales?
- What happened after the first attempts to free the whales failed?

Across Selections

- How is "The Story of Three Whales" different from the other stories you have read? How is it the same?

Beyond the Selection

- Do you know any other true stories where people were kind to animals? What happened?
- Think about how "The Story of the Three Whales" adds to what you know about kindness.
- Add items to the Concept/Question Board about kindness.

Cinderella

retold by Fabio Coen

illustrated by Lane Yerkes

Once there was a girl who was very kind and patient. Her wicked stepmother called her Cinderella because she often sat by the fireplace close to the cinders.

Her stepmother made her work all day long. She had to light the fire, prepare the meals, wash the dishes, clean the house, and make beautiful gowns for her two stepsisters, who were very ugly and very mean.

Cinderella was always dressed in rags, but she was more beautiful in her rags than her stepsisters in their beautiful gowns.

One day the King and Queen gave a ball. Cinderella helped her stepmother and her stepsisters to get ready. Then the three of them went to the ball.

Cinderella was all alone. She began to cry. Suddenly her Fairy Godmother appeared. "Why are you crying?" she asked Cinderella.

"I, too, would have liked to go to the ball," Cinderella replied.

"Then you shall go," said her Fairy Godmother. "Bring me a pumpkin from the garden."

With one touch of her magic wand, Cinderella's Fairy Godmother turned the pumpkin into a beautiful carriage. Then she took six mice from a trap. A touch of the magic wand turned them into six prancing horses. In the cellar Cinderella's Fairy Godmother found a large rat. She turned him into a large coachman with a great mustache.

Another touch of the magic wand and Cinderella's rags turned into a beautiful silver gown covered with diamonds. On her feet were a pair of little glass slippers.

As she stepped into the carriage, her Fairy Godmother said, "Have a good time, but remember this. You must leave the ball before midnight. When the clock strikes twelve, your carriage will turn into a pumpkin, your horses into mice, your coachman into a rat, and your gown into rags."

Cinderella promised to leave the ball before midnight. Then they drove away.

Cinderella was so beautiful that the prince danced with her all night. She forgot about her Fairy Godmother's warning. The clock began to strike twelve. Cinderella ran out of the palace and down the stairs. In her hurry she lost one of her glass slippers.

The prince ran after Cinderella, but it was too late. By the time he reached the bottom of the stairs, her beautiful carriage was gone. The prince found only her little glass slipper.

The prince had fallen in love with Cinderella. He wanted to find her, but he didn't even know her name or where she lived. He sent a page to every house in the kingdom. In each house the page asked every girl to try on the slipper. But their feet were much too big for the tiny slipper.

At last the page came to the house where Cinderella lived. Her two stepsisters hurried to try on the little slipper. But their feet were much too big. No matter how hard they tried, they could not get the slipper on.

Then it was Cinderella's turn. The slipper fit her perfectly. At that moment her Fairy Godmother appeared and dressed Cinderella in a gown of shimmering gold.

Cinderella and the prince were married. Because she was so kind, Cinderella forgave her wicked stepmother and stepsisters, and they all lived happily ever after.

Cinderella

Meet the Author

Fabio Coen was born in Rome, Italy. He came to the United States in 1940 and later became a citizen. He loved books and went to work for a publishing company. While he worked there he helped other authors of children's books get started.

Meet the Illustrator

Lane Yerkes has created illustrations for advertising, newspapers, magazines, textbooks, and logos. He has written and illustrated two children's stories that he hopes to publish. His home is located on the southwest coast of Florida, just above the Everglades. He lives with his wife and their dog. When not working, he enjoys boating and fishing.

Theme Connections

Within the Selection

Writer's Notebook Record your answers to the questions below in the Response Journal section of your Writer's Notebook. In small groups, report the ideas you wrote. Discuss your ideas with the rest of the group. Then choose a person to report your group's answers to the class.

- Why do you think Cinderella's stepmother and stepsisters were so mean to her?

- How was kindness shown to Cinderella?

- How did Cinderella show kindness?

Across Selections

- How is the Fairy Godmother in this story like the stranger in "The Paper Crane"?

- Do you think "Cinderella" and "Mufaro's Beautiful Daughters" are the same stories? How are they alike and different?

Beyond the Selection

- Do you think it is hard to be kind to people who are not kind to you? Why or why not?

- Add items to the Concept/Question Board about kindness.

Look Again

Seeing is believing. Or is it? Can you always trust what you see? Can something look like one thing and really be something different? Maybe!

Focus Questions Why do animals need to hide?
What does "there's more to the animal world
than meets the eye" mean?

I See Animals Hiding

by Jim Arnosky

I see animals hiding. I see a porcupine high in a tree.

Wild animals are shy and always hiding. It is natural for them to be this way. There are many dangers in the wild.

Even when they are caught unaware out in the open, wild animals try to hide. They stay behind whatever is available—a thin tree trunk or even a single blade of grass. Most of the time they go unnoticed.

The colors of wild animals match the colors of the places where the animals live. Because of this protective coloration, called camouflage, wild animals can hide by simply staying still and blending in.

Woodcocks and other birds, which spend much of their time on the woodland floor, have patterns and colors like those of dry leaves.

I see animals hiding. I see two woodcocks on the leafy ground.

Of all wild animals, deer are the wariest. Even though their colors are camouflaged, they feel safe only where there are good hiding places nearby.

In a summer meadow of tall grasses and small shrubby trees, deer can hide quickly by just lying down.

There are 20 deer on the snowy hill.
Can you find them all?

In autumn, deer shed their red-brown summer coats and replace them with warmer, grayer winter coats that better match the gray and brown trunks of leafless trees.

I see animals hiding. I see a whole herd of deer on a winter hill.

Snowshoe hares change from summer brown to winter white. The only way to spot a snowshoe hare in a snowy scene is to look for its shiny black eyes.

Squint your eyes and you will see just how invisible a snowshoe hare on snow can be.

Here are three more animals that are as white as snow. The arctic fox and long-tailed weasel change from winter white to summer brown. The snowy owl stays white year-round.

The colors and patterns of screech owls blend perfectly with tree bark. These small owls can sleep all day out in the open and not be discovered.

Besides an owl, there is one other bark imitator on this tree. Can you tell what it is?

I see animals hiding. I see an owl and a moth on a limb.

Trout are camouflaged by color and shape to blend with the smooth mossy stones in a stream.

Looking down in a brook, I see a speckled trout swimming amid speckled stones.

I see animals hiding. I see a garter snake slithering through the grass.

Up close a snake in the grass may be easy to see. But as long as the snake keeps a safe distance from its enemies, it can sneak by, looking like just another broken branch on the ground.

Stand back a few steps from this page, and using only your eyes, try to follow the line of the snake from its head to its tail. Can you tell what is snake and what is stick?

A bittern is a wading bird whose brown streaks and long sticklike legs naturally blend in with the cattails and reeds that grow along shorelines.

When a bittern really needs to be invisible, it points its bill upward and sways its long neck, like a cattail swaying gently in a breeze.

And last but not least:
Animals hide by staying inside.

I See Animals Hiding

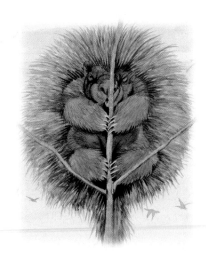

Meet the Author and Illustrator

James Edward Arnosky and his family live in the northern Vermont wilderness. He observes nature while fishing, drawing, or walking. His illustrations try to teach readers how to see as an artist would.

"I write about the world I live in and try to share all I see and feel in my books." Arnosky often describes the natural world in a way that the reader becomes a part of the scene. He sums up the role of an author saying, *"The best nonfiction lets the reader knock on the door, and you let them in. Then you go away."*

Theme Connections

Within the Selection

Writer's Notebook Record your answers to the questions below in the Response Journal section of your Writer's Notebook. In small groups, report the ideas you wrote. Discuss your ideas with the rest of the group. Then choose a person to report your group's answers to the class.

- Why is it sometimes difficult to spot animals in a natural setting?

- Why do animals need to hide?

Beyond the Selection

- What other things can you think of that you have to look closely at to really see?

- Think about what "I See Animals Hiding" tells you about camouflage.

- Add items to the Concept/Question Board about camouflage.

They Thought They Saw Him

Craig Kee Strete

illustrated by José Aruego and Ariane Dewey

● ●

Little dark chameleon crept out of the heart of his winter home and moved up onto a tiny branch.

Rain puddles glistened beneath his feet. The wind blew warm over the walls of the adobe. All winter little dark chameleon had lived, safe and asleep, beneath the granary where the people kept their seed corn.

Now insects buzzed over bush and tree, and he was awake.

As he moved on quick, silent feet, he began to forget the sleepy winter dark and felt now the joy in the first wakeful light of spring.

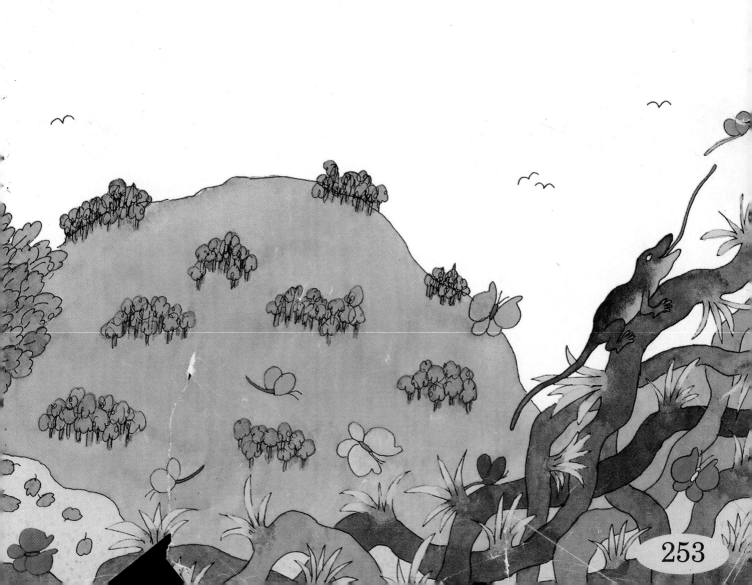

Eyes half closed, still filled with winter memories, little dark chameleon sat on a brown branch and waited for an insect to find his tongue.

A hungry snake watched him. The snake climbed the tree to catch the dark chameleon for his first meal of the spring.

But when he got there, everything on the brown branch was brown.

"The dark chameleon got away," said the snake, and he slithered off.

Little brown chameleon jumped off the brown branch. His feet gripped green leaves, and he hung there. His sticky tongue caught a bug.

An owl, flying home to sleep, saw the brown chameleon in the green leaves. The owl swooped down to catch him.

But when he got there, everything in the green leaves was green.

"The brown chameleon got away," hooted the owl, and he flew off.

Little green chameleon jumped out of the green leaves and landed softly in the tan, rain-washed sand.

A fox saw the green chameleon in the sand. With pointed ears and hungry eyes, the fox crept toward him.

But when he got there, everything in the tan sand was tan.

"The green chameleon got away," yipped the fox, and he ran off.

Little tan chameleon crawled up on a ridge of golden rock.

An Apache boy saw the tan chameleon and tried to sneak up and catch him for a spring surprise.

But when he got there, everything on the golden rock was golden.

"The tan chameleon got away," said the boy, and he slowly walked off.

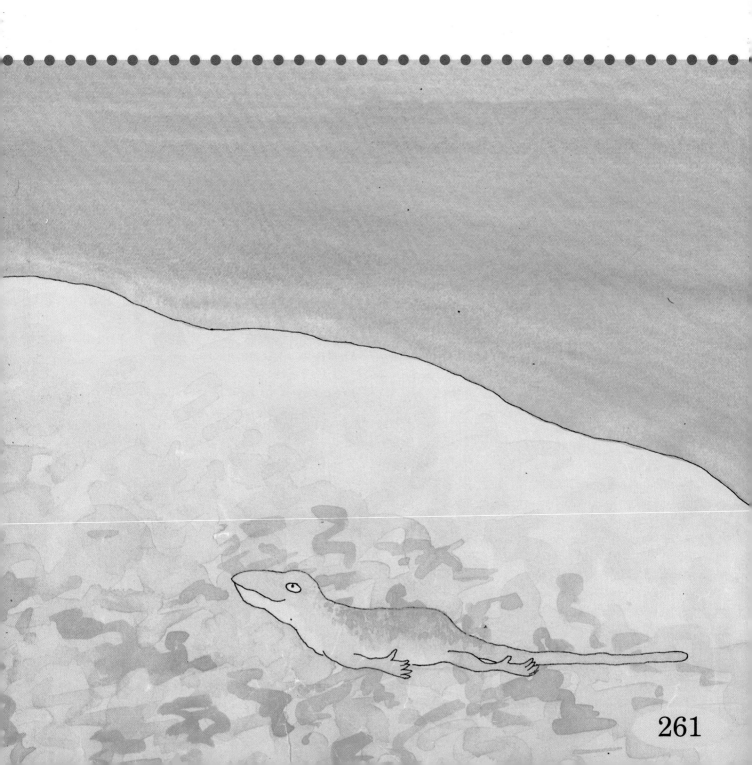

Little winter-dark, brown, green, tan, and golden chameleon warmed himself in the sunlight.

Snake, owl, fox, and boy all thought they saw him.

But little chameleon had his secret.

"Nobody sees me," he said, "because I am the color of the world."

They Thought They Saw Him

Meet the Author

Craig Kee Strete writes fiction for children and adults. He also writes for theater, television, and film. Strete's writing often describes the lives of young Native Americans growing up between two cultures. He shows the culture of the Native Americans and their love of nature. "They Thought They Saw Him" is a story that introduces Strete's world to others.

Meet the Illustrators

José Aruego and Ariane Dewey have combined their talents and have illustrated more than sixty children's books. Mr. Aruego does the drawings and Ms. Dewey adds the color through paint.

José Aruego began a career in law, but after a few months he realized that he wanted to draw, not practice law. After graduating from art school, he began drawing cartoons and later began illustrating children's books.

Ariane Dewey always loved bright colors. In fourth grade art class, she painted bright pink kids swimming in a blue-green lake. Her love of joyful colors is seen in many children's books.

Theme Connections

Within the Selection

Writer's Notebook Record your answers to the questions below in the Response Journal section of your Writer's Notebook. In small groups, report the ideas you wrote. Discuss your ideas with the rest of the group. Then choose a person to report your group's answers to the class.

• Why did the snake, owl, fox, and boy all think the chameleon got away?

• What was the chameleon's secret?

Across Selections

• Compare how a chameleon and a snowshoe hare use camouflage.

• Why can't a screech owl hide in as many places as a chameleon?

Beyond the Selection

• Think about how "They Thought They Saw Him" adds to what you know about camouflage.

• Add items to the Concept/Question Board about camouflage.

The Chameleon

John Gardner
illustrated by Susan Nethery

People say the Chameleon can take on
   the hue
   Of whatever he happens to be on.
   It's true
—Within reason, of course. If you put him on
   plaid
Or polka dots, he really gets mad.

Caterpillar

Christina Rossetti
illustrated by Susan Nethery

Brown and furry
   Caterpillar in a hurry,
   Take your walk
To the shady leaf, or stalk,
Or what not,
Which may be the chosen spot.
No toad spy you,
Hovering bird of prey pass by you;
Spin and die,
To live again a butterfly.

HUNGRY LITTLE HARE

by Howard Goldsmith
illustrated by Denny Bond

Little Hare the jackrabbit had great long ears with little black tips. Her long furry hind paws helped her hop very fast and jump very high.

268

One beautiful day, Little Hare smelled raspberries. Raspberry leaves were her favorite food.

Little Hare hopped, and then she hopped again. She followed the scent of raspberry to a pond in the meadow.

"Ouch!" a voice cried. "You stepped on me!"
Little Hare looked, but she saw only bright
green grass.

"I can't see you," Little Hare said.

"You're not supposed to see me," said a
green frog, hopping in front of Little Hare.
"My color hides me in the grass from
snoopy snakes. *You* don't eat frogs, do
you?"

"Oh, no!" said Little Hare. "I'm looking for raspberry leaves."

Little Hare hopped, and then she hopped
again. *Crunch, crunch, crunch* went the
twigs in the woods.

"Ouch!" a voice cried. "You pushed me!"

Little Hare looked, but she saw only brown
twigs on a tree stump.

"I can't see you," Little Hare said.

"You're not supposed to see me," said a walkingstick, crawling up to Little Hare. "I look exactly like a twig. That's how I hide from sneaky squirrels."

Little Hare was hungry. She hopped, and then she hopped again, past a big green bush.

"Ouch!" a voice said. "You bumped me!"

Little Hare looked, but she saw only slender green leaves.

"I can't see you," Little Hare said.

"You're not supposed to see me!" A katydid hopped up right in front of Little Hare. "I look exactly like a leaf, but I'm really an insect. My disguise protects me from prying praying mantises."

Now Little Hare was *very* hungry. She hopped, and then hopped again, and leaned against a tree to rest.

"Ouch!" said a voice. "Don't lean on me!"

Little Hare looked and looked, but she saw
only brown bark on the tree.

"I can't see you," said Little Hare. "I guess you look like something else, too."

"That's right," said a moth, fluttering in front of Little Hare. "My color matches the bark of a tree, so when I rest the wily woodpeckers can't find me."

Little Hare was just about to hop off when a
drowsy voice exclaimed, "Careful! I'm
resting in the leaves at your feet!"

Little Hare looked down just as a woodcock shook out his feathers.

"I blend into the leaves on the ground to avoid furry foxes," he explained.

Little Hare was so hungry she could barely
hop. But she spied some lovely lilies nearby.

She was just about to sniff them when a voice cried, "Don't sneeze!"

Little Hare looked, but she saw only yellow lilies.

"I can't see you," Little Hare said.

"You're not supposed to see me," replied a crab spider. "Leaping lizards think I'm a flower, but I only look like one. I can change color to match many kinds of flowers, so I'm invisible wherever I go."

"Well, I'm just a jackrabbit," said Little Hare,
"and I'm going to find my mother."

Soon Little Hare found her mother among tender, juicy raspberry leaves!

"Mother, what does *invisible* mean?" asked Little Hare as she munched.

"It means you disappear into the world around you," explained her mother.

"I wish I were invisible like the other animals and insects," said Little Hare.

"You will be," replied her mother. "You only have to wait."

And Mother Hare was right!

HUNGRY LITTLE HARE

Meet the Author

Howard Goldsmith was a psychologist before he was a children's author. He likes to make his books fun and challenging for his readers. His book, *2000 A.D.* is an adventure story. This is a good story for children who like to watch television space shows and movies. Grown-ups enjoy reading Goldsmith's books too.

Meet the Illustrator

Denny Bond has been an illustrator for many years. In addition to children's books, he has done illustrations for magazines, advertisements, and businesses. He is also a painter and has shown his paintings in art shows and at galleries. He tells young artists, *"dream with your eyes open…and always carry paper and pencil for doodling, or at least to write down ideas that may pop into your head…"*

Theme Connections

Within the Selection

Writer's Notebook Record your answers to the questions below in the Response Journal section of your Writer's Notebook. In small groups, report the ideas you wrote. Discuss your ideas with the rest of the group. Then choose a person to report your group's answers to the class.

- Why wasn't Little Hare able to see the other animals and insects?

- How was Little Hare able to become invisible?

Across Selections

- How were the animals and insects in this story like the chameleon in "They Thought They Saw Him"?

Beyond the Selection

- Have you ever not seen something because it was hidden? What was it?

- Think about how "Hungry Little Hare" adds to what you know about camouflage.

- Add items to the Concept/Question Board about camouflage.

Exotic Landscape. 1910. **Henri Rousseau.** Oil on canvas.
Norton Simon Foundation, Pasadena, California.

Printed Fabric from Bambalulu Handcraft Center. 1993. **Artist unknown.** Cotton with gold fabric ink. $2 \times 2\frac{1}{2}$ feet. Private Collection.

Deidre. 1982. **Wendy Fay Dixon.** Silverpoint on paper. $17\frac{3}{4} \times 17$ in. The National Museum of Women in the Arts, Washington, D.C.

How to Hide an Octopus
& other sea creatures

by Ruth Heller

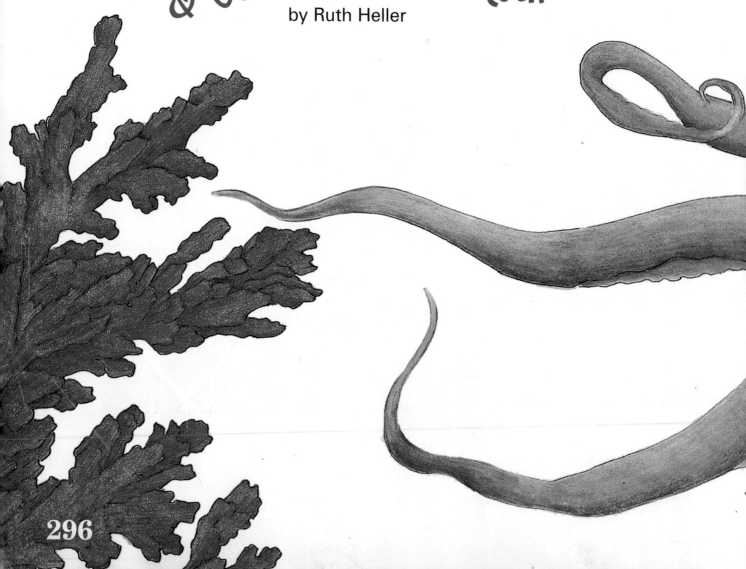

If
you take
a careful look,
you'll see
how
creatures
in this book
are
CAMOUFLAGED
and out
of view—
although
they're right
in front
of you.

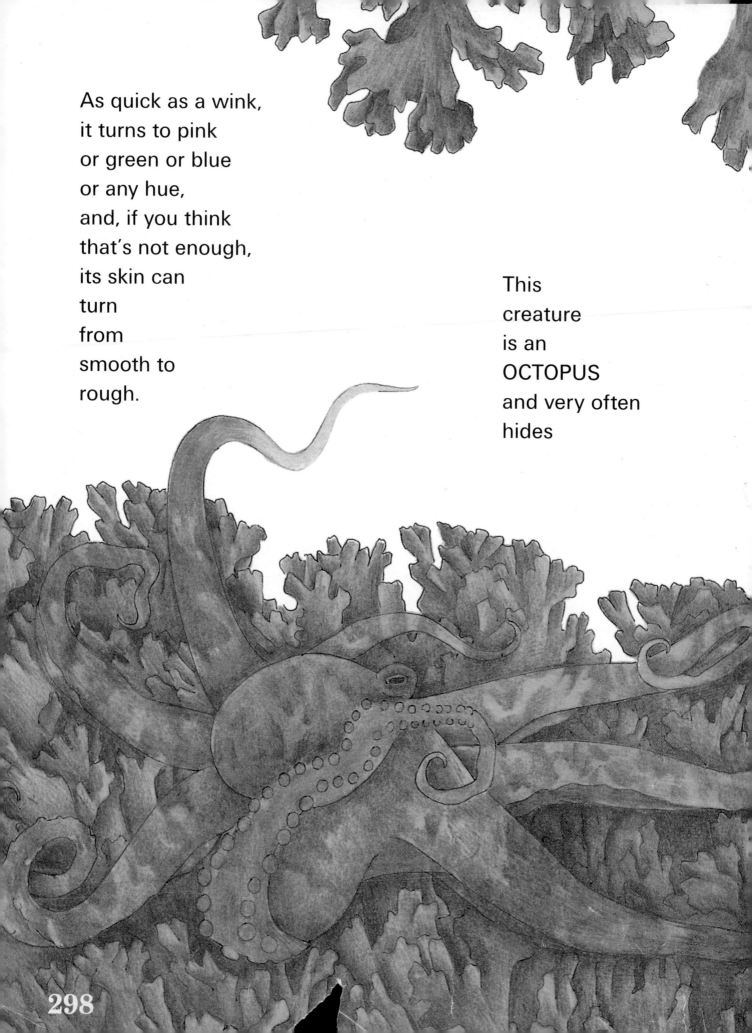

As quick as a wink,
it turns to pink
or green or blue
or any hue,
and, if you think
that's not enough,
its skin can
turn
from
smooth to
rough.

This
creature
is an
OCTOPUS
and very often
hides

by
changing
to the
color . . .

over
which
it glides.

Its relative,
the
CUTTLEFISH,
could do the same
if he should wish.

The stripes that he is
sporting
show
that he's
been courting,
but
he can
make them
fade away . . .

slowly
or
without
delay.

The
SARGASSUM FISH,
grotesque
at
best,
looks
just
like . . .

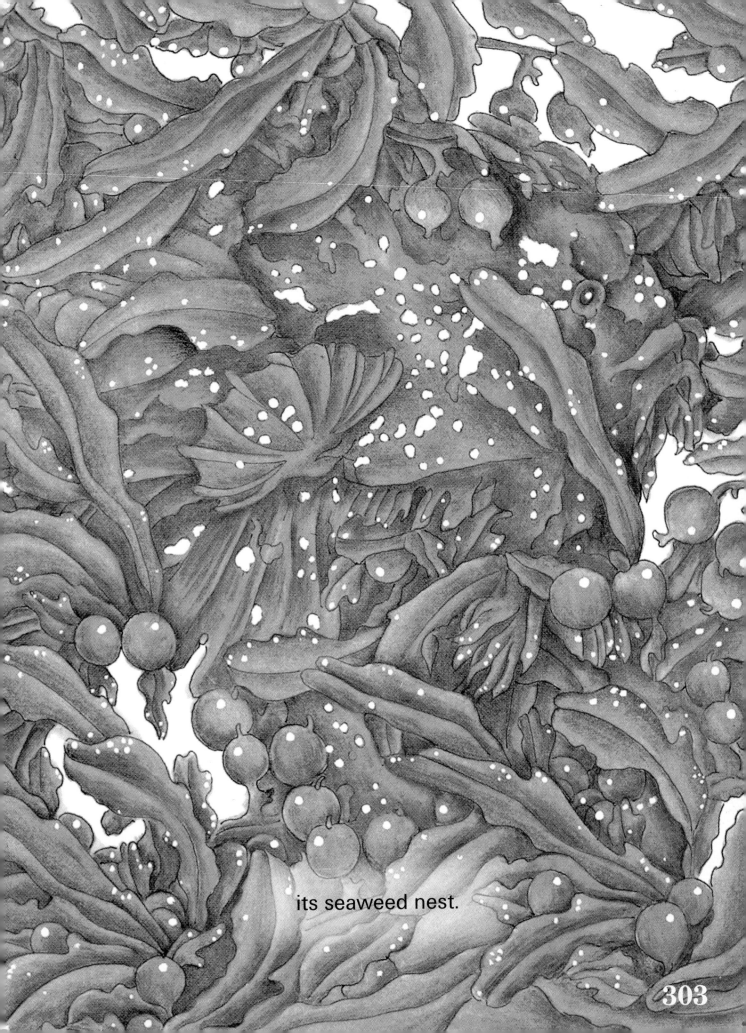

its seaweed nest.

The
giant red
SEA DRAGON
is
the most bizarre
of all the
creatures
seen so far,
with
ribbons of skin
that grow
from its chin
and
from its
belly and back.

They
spread
from its head
and trail from its tail,
and it's
easy to see
why its enemies fail
to find
where it feeds . . .

among the red weeds.

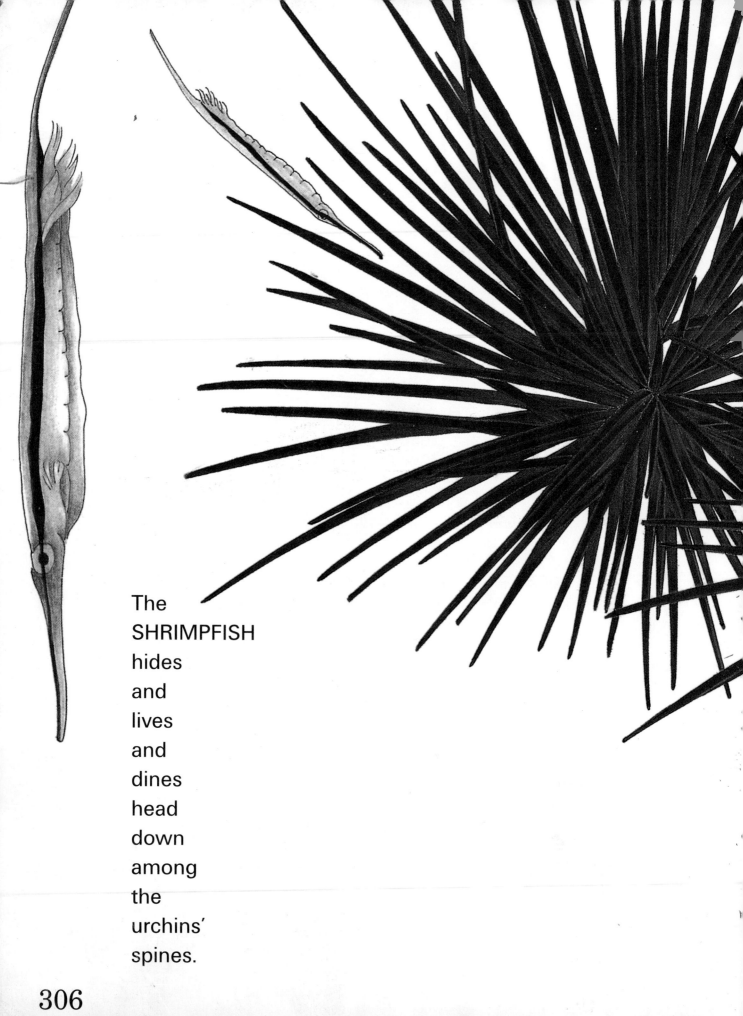

The
SHRIMPFISH
hides
and
lives
and
dines
head
down
among
the
urchins'
spines.

Heads
up,
the
PIPEFISH
like
to
play
and
with
the
grasses
drift
and
sway.

307

The
BUTTERFLY
FISH

has been
designed

to
make
it
very
hard . . .

to
find.

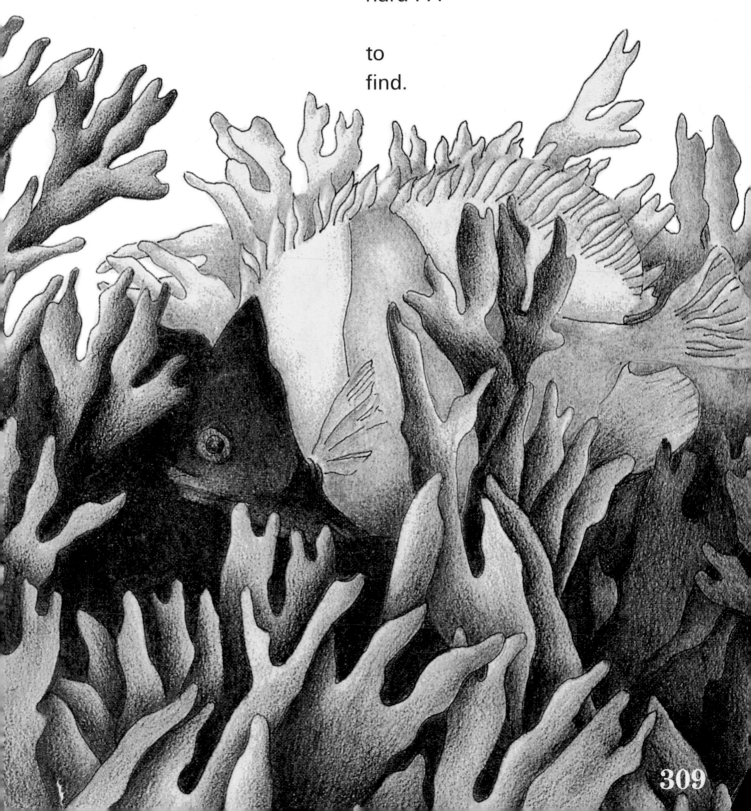

The
DECORATOR CRAB
is drab
and
will not rest
until it's dressed,

so
it proceeds
to don
some
weeds
and barnacles
and sponge,
you
see,

and
even
an . . .
anemone.

311

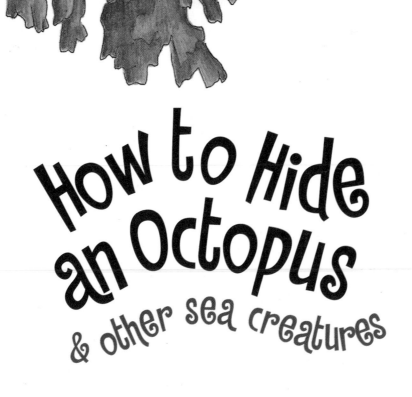

How to Hide an Octopus

& other sea creatures

Meet the Author

Ruth Heller is a writer and an illustrator. She began her career designing wrapping paper, napkins, kites, mugs, and greeting cards. She even designed coloring books. Once when she was studying tropical fish for a coloring book that she was making, Ruth Heller saw a strange looking shape floating in the fish tank. It was an egg sac. Heller began to read about egg-laying animals. She thought about the egg in the fish tank. Colorful shapes and words began to go through her mind. That was when Ruth Heller decided to write and illustrate children's books. Her first book was called *Chickens Aren't the Only Ones*.

Theme Connections

Within the Selection

Writer's Notebook Record your answers to the questions below in your Response Journal section of your Writer's Notebook. In small groups, report the ideas you wrote. Discuss your ideas with the rest of your group. Then choose a person to report your group's answers to the class.

- How does an octopus hide?
- Why are the sea creatures in this story camouflaged?

Across Selections

- How is "How to Hide an Octopus and Other Sea Creatures" like the other stories you have read? How is it different?

Beyond the Selection

- Think about how "How to Hide an Octopus and Other Sea Creatures" adds to what you know about camouflage.
- Add items to the Concept/Question Board about camouflage.

How the Guinea Fowl Got Her Spots

retold and illustrated by Barbara Knutson

A long time ago, when everything had just been made, Nganga the Guinea Fowl had glossy black feathers all over. She had no white speckles as she does today—not a single spot.

314

Guinea Fowl was a little bird, but she had a big friend. And that was Cow.

They liked to go to the great green hills where Cow could eat grass and Nganga could scratch for seeds and crunch grasshoppers.

And they would both keep an eye out for Lion.

One day, Guinea Fowl was crossing the river to meet Cow on the most delicious hill they knew. The grass was so juicy and thick that, even from the river, Nganga could hear Cow hungrily tearing up one mouthful after another.

But . . . what was that Nganga saw slinking toward Cow?

Was it . . . ?

Yes, it was LION!

Now you might think a guinea fowl is no match for a lion, but Nganga didn't think that. In fact, she didn't think at all.

She scratched and scrambled up the bank as fast as she could and whirred right between Cow and Lion, kicking and flapping in the dust.

"RAAUGH!" shouted Lion.

"My eyes! This sand! What was that?"

When the clouds of dust thinned there was
no sign of anyone—certainly not any dinner
for Lion. He went home in a terrible temper,
growling like his empty belly.

The next day, Guinea Fowl was at the grassy patch first. You can be sure she had her eyes wide open for Lion.

Soon she saw Cow cautiously crossing the river to join her—shlip, clop, shlop. But something yellow was twitching in the reeds.

Wasn't that Lion's tail?

Up whirred Nganga, half tumbling, half flying with her stubby wings. Lion looked up, startled, from his hiding place. Frrrr . . . a little black whirlwind was racing across the grass toward the river. "Whe-klo-klo-klo!" it called out to Cow.

"Guinea Fowl! That's where the duststorm came from yesterday," growled Lion between his sharp teeth. But the next moment, the whirlwind hit the river.

"RAAUghmf!" Lion exploded with a roar that ended underwater.

"I'll teach that bird to chase away my dinner!" he spluttered. But by the time his roar was working properly again, Cow and Guinea Fowl were safely over the next hill at Cow's house.

"Nganga," mooed Cow gratefully, "twice you have helped me escape from Lion. Now I will help you do the same."

Turning around, she dipped her tasseled tail into a calabash of milk. Then she shook the tasselful of milk over Guinea Fowl's sleek black feathers—flick, flock, flick—spattering her with creamy white milk.

Guinea Fowl craned her head and admired the delicate speckles covering her back.

She spread her wings, and Cow sprinkled them with milk too—flick, flock, flick.

"Whe-klo-klo! That's beautiful, Cow!" chuckled Nganga. "Thank you, my friend!"

And she set off for home.

Whom should she meet where the path crossed the river but Lion, still shaking the water out of his ears and angrier than ever.

"Ho, Speckled Bird!" snorted Lion. "Have you seen Guinea Fowl on your path?"

"Oh yes," clucked Nganga, hiding a smile. "I believe she went that way."

She pointed with her spotted wing to the hills far down the river.

"If you go quickly and don't stop to rest, you may catch up with her in a few days."

Lion leaped up at once, not bothering to thank the strange bird. A minute later, he thought about taking her along for a traveling snack, but when he looked back at the riverbank, he could see no trace of her.

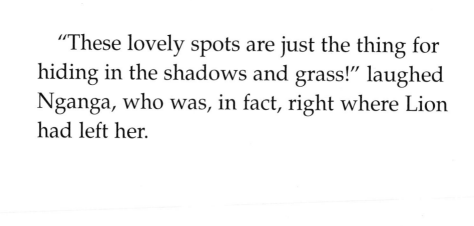

"These lovely spots are just the thing for hiding in the shadows and grass!" laughed Nganga, who was, in fact, right where Lion had left her.

And she turned back to Cow's house to thank her friend again.

How the Guinea Fowl Got Her Spots

Meet the Author and Illustrator

Barbara Knutson was born in South Africa. She studied art in Africa and the United States. After receiving a degree in art education and French, she taught English and French in an international school in Nigeria.

Having grown up in South Africa and having traveled in other African countries, Barbara Knutson has a lot of personal experiences to use in her illustrations. Her detailed watercolors show the love and knowledge she has of African culture. She now lives in Minnesota where she visits schools and works at a children's bookstore.

Theme Connections

Within the Selection

Writer's Notebook Record your answers to the questions below in the Response Journal section of your Writer's Notebook. In small groups, report the ideas you wrote. Discuss your ideas with the rest of the group. Then choose a person to report your group's answers to the class.

- How did Guinea Fowl protect her friend Cow from Lion?

- How did Cow help protect Guinea Fowl?

Across Selections

- How is the way that camouflage helped Guinea Fowl the same as how camouflage helped animals in other stories?

- How is this story like "Mushroom in the Rain"?

Beyond the Selection

- Think about how "How the Guinea Fowl Got Her Spots" adds to what you know about camouflage.

- Add items to the Concept/Question Board about camouflage.

Focus Questions Why do animals camouflage themselves in different ways? How is camouflage like wearing a costume?

Animal Camouflage

by Janet McDonnell

What Is Camouflage?

Have you ever played hide and seek outside? Sometimes it is hard to find a good place to hide! But what if you could paint yourself brown and green like the ground?

Or put on a costume that made you look like a tree? Or lie down and cover yourself with leaves? All of these tricks would make you much harder to find.

A forest looks green and brown.

What Is Camouflage?

Some animals use tricks to hide themselves. Using colors and patterns to hide is called camouflage. Camouflage makes things very hard to find—even when they are out in the open.

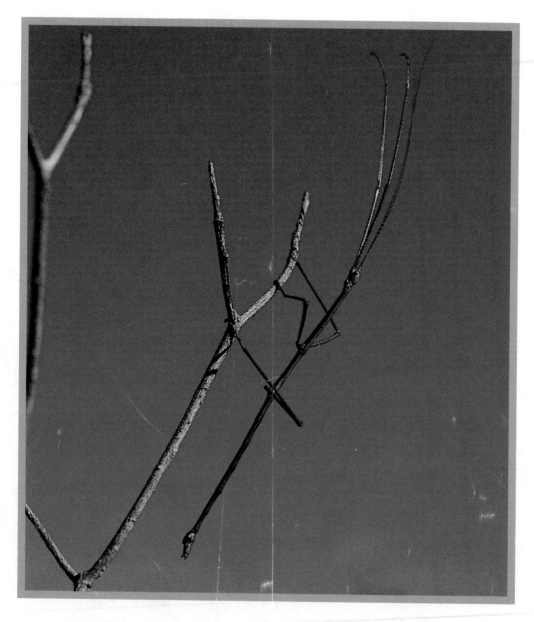

A walkingstick looks like the branches around it.

Animals, fish, reptiles, and even people use camouflage for hiding. When something looks like the objects around it, it is much harder to see. That is what camouflage is all about!

Why Do Animals Need Camouflage?

There are many reasons why animals hide. They often hide from their enemies. Some animals move around at night and sleep during the day. They need to stay hidden while they sleep.

This emperor moth has an eyespot on its wing to scare enemies.

Other animals hide so that they can be better hunters. Camouflage helps them sneak up on their dinner.

How Do Animals Use Camouflage?

Animals use camouflage in many different ways. Some use it to blend in with the objects around them. These objects are called surroundings. The *polar bear's* white coat blends in with its surroundings—the white snow. This color hides the bear when it is hunting for seals.

The white fur of this polar bear looks like the snow around it.

The *black bear's* dark coat helps it hide in dark trees and bushes.

But what happens if an animal's surroundings are more than one color? Some animals have camouflage with more than one color, too!

Some fish have dark backs and white bellies. When a hungry bird looks into the dark water, the fish's dark back is hard to see. But to an enemy deeper in the water, the fish's white belly blends in with the bright sky.

This large mouth bass has a dark back that matches the water.

Why Do Some Animals Change Color?

Sometimes an animal's surroundings change. Then the animal has to change color, too! That is the only way it can stay hidden. Some animals change color to match the season. The *snowshoe rabbit* changes color very slowly in the spring and fall.

In the winter, the snowshoe rabbit's fur is white like the snow. As the snow melts in the spring, the rabbit grows patches of brown fur. It looks just like patches of ground and melting snow.

This snowshoe rabbit has white fur to match the snow.

Then summer comes, and the ground is brown. The rabbit's fur grows brown to match. When fall comes, the rabbit starts to turn white again.

This baby snowshoe rabbit has brown fur in the spring.

Do All Animals Use Colors to Hide?

Some animals use designs, or patterns, instead of changing colors. Blending into a pattern is a good way to hide. When an animal's body looks like its surroundings, it is very hard to find.

A *fawn*, or baby deer, is too weak to run fast. But it can hide by lying still. The fawn's back is covered with dots. The dots look like spots of sunlight on the forest floor. If the fawn stays still, it is very hard to see.

Fawns like this one can blend into their surroundings.

Another animal that uses patterns to hide is the *bittern*. This bird lives in marshes with tall grass. The stripes on its feathers look just like shadows in the grass.

This bittern has patterns that match the tall grass.

When the bittern is in danger, it makes itself even harder to find. It points its beak straight up and sways its body in the breeze. The bittern looks just like the blowing grass!

What Is Mimicry?

Some animals have a shape or color that looks like something else. This type of camouflage is called mimicry. Animals that use mimicry are good pretenders.

The *walkingstick* is one insect that uses mimicry. Its long, thin, bumpy body looks just like a small branch!

This walkingstick looks like a branch.

Walkingsticks can even change color with the seasons. In the spring, the tree's branches and leaves are green. The walkingstick is green, too. When the branches and leaves turn brown, the walkingstick turns brown to match.

Some animals use other kinds of mimicry to fool their enemies. Some moths have large spots on their rear wings. The spots look just like eyes!

When the moth is resting, its front wings cover the spots. But when the moth senses danger, it lifts its front wings and shows the spots. If an enemy is afraid of the big "eyes," it will leave the moth alone.

The spots on this lo moth's wings look like eyes.

Some animals even make their own
costumes for camouflage. The *masked crab*
uses seaweed to make a costume.

This masked crab has used many things to make
its costume.

First the crab uses its claws to tear the seaweed into pieces. Then it puts each piece in its mouth and chews it until it is soft. The crab sticks the pieces of seaweed to itself. Little hooks on its shell and legs hold the seaweed in place.

From a rabbit that changes color to a crab in a seaweed costume, there are many kinds of camouflage. But each kind of camouflage has the same important job—to help animals hide.

This zale moth is hard to see because it looks like the tree trunk.

Now that you know some of their tricks,
maybe you will see animals where you never
saw them before. But you'll have to look
very carefully, or you might be fooled!

Animal Camouflage

Meet the Author

Janet McDonnell came up with the idea for writing "Animal Camouflage" during a brainstorming session with publishers. Since she loves animals, she was excited to be given the chance to write about them. When she writes about a subject, she likes to research it very carefully. Sometimes she gets so much information that she cannot use it because the book can only be so long. Then her challenge is to get the ideas across in a clear and interesting way. *"My goal is to make the reader as excited about the topic as I am,"* she said.

Theme Connections

Within the Selection

Writer's Notebook Record your answers to the questions below in the Response Journal section of your Writer's Notebook. In small groups, report the ideas you wrote. Discuss your ideas with the rest of the group. Then choose a person to report your group's answers to the class.

- What are some of the different ways that animals use camouflage?

- Why do some animals have so much color or have special markings?

- Which animals were the most difficult to find in the photographs?

Across Selections

- How many different kinds of camouflage can you name from the stories we've read? Give examples from the stories.

Beyond the Selection

- Where have you noticed animals using camouflage? Did you have to look very carefully to find them?

- Think about how "Animal Camouflage" adds to what you know about camouflage.

- Add items to the Concept/Question Board about camouflage.

Pronunciation Key

a as in **a**t

ā as in l**a**te

â as in c**a**re

ä as in f**a**ther

e as in s**e**t

ē as in m**e**

i as in **i**t

ī as in k**i**te

o as in **o**x

ō as in r**o**se

ô as in b**ou**ght and r**aw**

oi as in c**oi**n

o͝o as in b**oo**k

ōo as in t**oo**

or as in f**or**m

ou as in **ou**t

u as in **u**p

ū as in **u**se

ûr as in t**ur**n; g**er**m, l**ear**n, f**ir**m, w**or**k

ə as in **a**bout, chick**e**n, penc**i**l, cann**o**n, circ**u**s

ch as in **ch**air

hw as in **wh**ich

ng as in ri**ng**

sh as in **sh**op

th as in **th**in

t͟h as in **th**ere

zh as in trea**s**ure

The mark (′) is placed after a syllable with a heavy accent, as in **chicken** (chik′ ən).

The mark (′) after a syllable shows a lighter accent, as in **disappear** (dis′ ə p ēr′).

Glossary

A

admire (ad mīr´) *v.* To be pleased with.

adobe (ə dō´ bē) *n.* A building made of brick or dried mud.

adrift (ə drift´) *adj.* Floating or moving without direction.

adventure (əd ven´ chər) *n.* A task or event that is likely to be exciting or dangerous.

amazement (ə māz´ mənt) *n.* Being very surprised and full of wonder.

amazing (ə mā´ zing) *adj.* Surprising; causing wonder.

amid (ə mid´) *prep.* In with; around; in the middle of.

anytime (en´ ē tīm´) *adv.* At any time.

Apache (ə pa´ chē) *adj.* Pertaining to a Native American group of the southwestern United States.

assistant (ə sis´ tənt) *n.* A helper; a person whose job is to help another person.

available (ə vā´ lə bəl) *adj.* Being in the area and ready to use.

avoid (ə void´) *v.* Stay away from.

B

ball (bôl) *n.* A large, fancy party at which people dance.

barely (bâr´ lē) *adv.* Only just; scarcely.

barnacles (bar´ nə kəlz) *n.* Small sea animals that have a shell and attach themselves to rocks, ship bottoms, and docks.

beard (bērd) *n.* Hair on a chin.

beautiful (bū´ tə fəl) *adj.* Pleasing to look at, hear, or think about.

bizarre (bi zar´) *adj.* Very unusual looking.

blend (blend) *v.* Mix together so as not to be seen.

bloom (blōōm) *n.* A large group of plankton on the ocean surface.

boring (bôr ing) *adj.* To make tired or restless by being dull.

brow (brou) *n.* Area including the eyebrows and forehead.

bulletin board (buˊ lə tən bord) *n.* A place on a wall for messages and other information.

butterfly (buˊ tûr flīˊ) *n.* An insect with a thin body and four large, often brightly colored wings. Butterflies fly in the daytime.

C

calabash (kaˊ lə bashˊ) *n.* A gourd with a hard shell that can be made into a dipper.

calm (käm) *adj.* Not excited or nervous; quiet.

camouflage (kamˊ ə fläzh) *adj.* Hard to see because it looks the same as the area around it.

cane (kān) *n.* A stick to help a person in walking.

cattail (katˊ tālˊ) *n.* A tall reedy plant with a fuzzy brown top that grows in very wet areas.

cautiously (kôˊ shəs lē) *adv.* With care; watching out for danger.

ceiling (sēˊ ling) *n.* The top of a room.

cellar (selˊ ər) *n.* A room underground.

chance (chans) *n.* A time for one to do something.

chatter (chaˊ tər) *v.* To click together quickly.

chrysalis (krisˊ ə lis) *n.* The protective covering around the butterfly larva when it is in the stage of changing into butterfly.

cinder (sinˊ dər) *n.* A small bit of coal or wood that has been burned until it is black.

clearing (klēr´ing) *n.* In a forest, a piece of land with no trees or bushes.

clearing

clever (kle´ vər) *adj.* Very smart.

coachman (kōch´ mən) *n.* A person who drives a carriage.

cobbler (kob´ lər) *n.* A person who makes and repairs shoes.

coloration (kə´ lə rā´ shən) *n.* The way something is colored.

concrete torpedo (kon´ krēt tor pē´ dō) *n.* A heavy block of stone used to hit something hard enough to make it break apart.

costume (kos´ to͞om´) *n.* Something put on to change the way one looks.

cot (kot) *n.* A small bed that usually can be folded.

courthouse (kort´ hous´) *n.* A building with courtrooms and offices.

court (kort´) *v.* Trying to find a mate.

crane (krān) *n.* A bird with a long neck, beak, and legs that lives near water.

crane (krān) *v.* To stretch out the neck in order to see better.

creature (krē´ chər) *n.* Any animal that is alive.

crept (krept) *v.* A past tense of **creep** (krēp) *v.* To move slowly and quietly.

crumpled (krum´ pəld) *adj.* Crushed and bent out of shape.

D

decorate (de´ kə rāt´) *v.* To add designs or pictures to make something look better.

delicious (di lish´ əs) *adj.* Pleasing or delightful to the taste or smell.

department (di pärt´ mənt) *n.* A single area of a store; a part of a store where one type of item is sold.

design (di zīn´) *v.* Make by following a plan.

diamond (dī´ mənd) *n.* A mineral that consists of pure carbon in the form of a clear or pale crystal. It is the hardest natural material known.

dine (dīn) *v.* To eat food.

disappear (dis´ ə pēr´) *v.* To no longer be seen.

disguise (dis gīz´) *n.* Anything that hides something from view.

don (don) *v.* To put on, like clothes.

donation (dō nā´ shən) *n.* Something given to a person or group.

drab (drab) *adj.* Plain and without color.

drenched (drenched) *v.* To make something completely wet.

drift (drift) *v.* To move because of a current of air or water.

droop (drōōp) *v.* To hang or sink down.

drowsy (drou´ zē) *adj.* Feeling sleepy.

E

eager (ē´ gər) *adj.* Looking forward to doing something.

elves (elvz) *n.* The plural of **elf:** A small fairy who sometimes plays tricks.

enemy (en´ ə mē) *n.* Animal that might cause harm.

enormous (i nôr´ məs) *adj.* Huge; very big.

escalator (es´ kə lā´ tər) *n.* A moving stairway.

exciting (eks sīt´ ing) *adj.* Causing excitement.

exclaim (iks klām´) *v.* To cry out suddenly.

F

fade (fād) *v.* Lose some of the color.

fasten (fas´ ən) *v.* To attach firmly.

fawn (fôn) *n.* A young deer.

fig (fig) *n.* A sweet fruit of a shrub or small tree that grows in warm regions. Figs have many tiny seeds, and are often preserved by drying.

finally (fī′ nəl lē) *adv.* At the end; at last.

flick (flik) *v.* To move in a rapid or jerky way.

forgave (fər gāv′) *v.* The past tense of **forgive**: To pardon; to excuse.

froth (frôth) *n.* Bubbles formed in a liquid; foamy liquid.

G

gasp (gasp) *v.* To breathe in gulps with the mouth wide open.

glare (glâr) *v.* To look at with anger.

glide (glīd) *v.* To move in a smooth and steady way.

glisten (gli′ sən) *v.* To shine or sparkle.

glossy (glo′ sē) *adj.* Having a shine or luster.

goddess (god′ is) *n.* A female god.

gown (goun) *n.* A woman's dress, often fancy.

granary (grā′ nə rē) *n.* A building in which grains, such as corn or wheat, are stored.

greedy (grē′ dē) *adj.* A very great and selfish desire for more than one's share.

grip (grip) *v.* To take hold of firmly and tightly.

grotesque (grō tesk′) *adj.* Odd or unusual looking.

guest (gest) *n.* A customer in a restaurant, hotel, or similar place.

guinea fowl (gi′ nē foul) *n.* An African bird that has a bare neck and head.

guinea fowl

Pronunciation Key: at; lāte; câre; fäther; set; mē; **it**; kīte; **ox**; rōse; ô in b**ought**; c**oin**; b**oo**k; t**oo**; f**orm**; **out**; **up**; use; tûrn; ə sound in **a**bout, chick**e**n, penc**i**l, cann**o**n, circ**u**s; **ch**air; **hw** in **wh**ich; ri**ng**; **sh**op; **th**in; **th**ere; **zh** in trea**s**ure.

gulp (gulp) *n.* To swallow large amounts of something all at one time.

H

handsome (han´ səm) *adj.* Having a pleasing appearance.

herd (hûrd) *n.* A group of animals.

host (hōst) *n.* The person who is taking care of guests.

hover (hu´ vər) *v.* To stay in one place while in the air.

howling (houl ing) *v.* To make a loud, wailing cry.

huddle (hud´ l) *v.* To crowd together; to wrap up tightly in.

hue (hū) *n.* Color.

I

ice-breaker (īs´ brā´ kər) *n.* A ship used to break a channel through ice.

ice-breaker

ice-pole (īs´ pōl) *n.* A metal pole with a pointed end used to chip ice.

imitator (i´ mə tā´ tər) *n.* One who copies something or someone.

incredible (in kred´ ə bəl) *adj.* Beyond belief.

Inuit (i´ nōō wət) *n.* People native to the northwestern part of North America and Arctic.

invincible (in´ vin´ sə bəl) *adj.* So strong that it cannot be beaten or broken.

invisible (in viz´ ə bəl) *adj.* Not able to be seen.

K

katydid (kā′ tē did′) *n.* A large, green grasshopper.

kingdom (king′ dəm) *n.* A country that is ruled by a king or a queen.

L

lad (lad) *n.* A male child; boy.

lap (lap) *v.* To drink by pulling liquid into the mouth with the tongue.

larva (lar′ və) *n.* The newly hatched form of some insects and other animals without backbones. A larva has a soft body that looks like a worm and has no wings. A caterpillar is the larva of a moth or butterfly, and a grub is the larva of a beetle.

lean (lēn) *v.* To sit with one's back resting against something.

leather (letℏ′ ər) *n.* The skin of an animal after it has been tanned, or softened; for use in making shoes and other items.

librarian (lī brâr′ ē ən) *n.* A person who is in charge of or works in a library.

library card (lī′ brâr′ ē kard) *n.* A card which lets you borrow library books.

lurk (lûrk) *v.* To move slowly and quietly without being noticed.

M

manner (ma′ nər) *n.* A way of acting or behaving.

marigold (mâr i gōld) *n.* A garden plant that bears yellow, orange, or red flowers in summer.

marsh (marsh) *n.* Low, wet land. Grasses and reeds grow in marshes.

meadow (med′ ō) *n.* A field of grass.

midnight (mid′ nīt′) *n.* Twelve o′clock at night; the middle of the night.

mimicry (mim′ i krē) *n.* Camouflage that makes an animal look like another kind of animal.

mistake (mi stāk´) *v.* Something that is not correctly done, said, or thought; error.

mystery (mis´ tə rē) *n.* Something that is not or cannot be known, explained, or understood.

N

natural (na´ chə rəl) *adj.* Acting on information one is born with.

nearsighted (nēr´ sī´ tid) *adj.* Not able to see things far away.

nectar (nek´ tûr) *n.* The sweet liquid formed in flowers. Bees use nectar to make honey.

nimble (nim´ bəl) *adj.* Able to move easily; light on one's feet.

O

olympiad (ō lim´ pē ad) *n.* A great contest.

ordeal (or dēl´) *v.* A stressful time or event.

overalls (ō´ vər ôlz´) *n.* Loose trousers with a bib front and straps at the shoulders.

overjoyed (ō´ vûr joid´) *adj.* Extremely happy.

P

pack-ice (pak´ īs´) *n.* Sea ice that forms when pieces of floating ice get crushed together.

page (pāj) *n.* A boy servant.

palace (pal´ is) *n.* A large, fancy house; the home of a king and queen.

parlor (par´ lər) *n.* A room for visiting with friends.

particular (pər ti´ kyə lər) *adj.* Being one single thing.

patient (pā´ shənt) *adj.* Calm; willing to wait; able to put up with a bad situation without complaining.

patterns (pat´ ərnz) *n.* Repeated shapes or colors on an animal.

perform (pər form´) *v.* To act, sing, or dance in front of others.

perspire (pər spīr´) *v.* To sweat.

persuade (pər swād´) *v.* To convince someone to do or believe something.

plaid (plad) *n.* A pattern of overlapping squares, rectangles, and lines.

plankton (plangk´ tən) *n.* A kind of very small plant life in a body of water.

plight (plīt) *n.* A bad situation.

plunge (plunj) *v.* To dive down into the water.

polish (po´ ləsh) *v.* To make smooth and shiny by rubbing.

polka dot (pō´ kə dot´) *n.* A pattern of solid colored circles.

praying mantis (prā´ ing man´ tis) *n.* Large, green insect that holds its front legs as if praying.

pretender (prē tend ûr) *v.* One who gives a false show.

promptly (prompt´ lē) *adv.* Quickly.

protect (prə tekt´) *v.* To keep from harm.

protective (prə tek´ tiv) *adj.* Keeps out of danger or away from harm.

prying (prī´ ing) *adj.* Being nosey.

pteranodon (tə ra´ nə don) *n.* A flying dinosaur.

Q

quickly (kwik´ lē) *adv.* Thinking, learning, or reacting easily and rapidly.

R

raid (rād) *n.* A sudden entering to take something.

ridge (rij) *n.* The long and narrow upper part of something

reply (ri plī´) *v.* To answer.

rounds (roundz) *n.* The same trip taken over and over; a route taken that begins each time in the same place.

> **Pronunciation Key:** at; lāte; câre; fäther; set; mē; it; kīte; ox; rōse; ô in bought; coin; bŏŏk; tōō; form; out; up; use; tûrn; ə sound in about, chicken, pencil, cannon, circus; chair; hw in which; ring; shop; thin; there; zh in treasure.

S

search (sûrch) *v.* To look for.

scent (sent) *n.* Smell.

scramble (skram´bəl) *v.* To move or climb quickly.

serve (serv) *v.* To bring food to.

shimmer (shim´ûr) *v.* To shine with a faint, flickering light; glimmer.

shoemaker (shōō´ mā´ kər) *n.* A person who makes or repairs shoes.

shopper (shop´ ər) *n.* A person who is looking for things to buy.

shrubby (shru´ bē) *adj.* Filled out with leaves and limbs; bushy.

sigh (sī) *v.* To let out a loud breath.

sky-crane (skī´ krān) *n.* A machine that uses cables to lift and move heavy objects.

slink (slingk) *v.* To move quietly, slowly, and close to the ground; to creep.

slither (slith´ ûr) *v.* To slide or glide like a snake.

sneaky (snē´ kē) *adj.* Trying to keep from being seen.

sniff (snif) *v.* To smell; to draw a short breath up the nose.

snoopy (snōō´ pē) *adj.* Looking for or prowling.

sofa (sō´ fə) *n.* A couch with a back and two arms.

spatter (spa´ tər) *v.* To splash with small drops.

spied (spīd) *v.* To notice.

splutter (splu´ tər) *v.* To say with a splashing sound.

sporting (spor´ ting) *v.* Showing.

squid (skwid) *n.* A sea animal with a tube-shaped body and ten arms.

squid

stacks (staks) *n.* Piles formed by putting books on top of each other.

stalk (stôk) *n.* The main stem of a plant.

stare (stâr) *v.* To look very hard or very long with the eyes wide open.

steadies (sted´ēs) *adj.* Firm in movement or position; not shaky.

steamer trunk (stē´ mər trungk) *n.* A big, strong box with a lid used for storage.

steep (stēp) *adj.* Almost straight up-and-down.

stranger (strān´ jûr) *n.* A person whom one does not know.

stubby (stu´ bē) *adj.* Short and thick.

supermarket (soo´ pər mär´ kət) *n.* A store in which a person can choose food and household items to buy.

surface (sûr´ fəs) *n.* The top part of something.—*v.* To come up to the surface.

surroundings (sə roun´ dingz) *n.* The objects around an animal.

swoop (swoop) *v.* To fly down then back up quickly.

T

tasseled (ta´ səld) *adj.* Looking like a tassel, which is a bunch of strings tied at one end.

temperature (tem´ pə chər´) *n.* A measure of how warm or cold something is.

tender (ten´ dər) *adj.* Soft and gentle.

thorny (thor´ nē) *adj.* Having a sharp point on a branch or stem.

> **Pronunciation Key: a**t; l**ā**te; c**â**re; f**ä**ther; s**e**t; m**ē**; **i**t; k**ī**te; **o**x; r**ō**se; **ô** in b**o**ught; **c**oin; b**oo**k; t**oo**; f**or**m; **ou**t; **u**p; **u**se; t**û**rn; **ə** sound in **a**bout, chick**e**n, penc**i**l, cann**o**n, circ**u**s; **ch**air; **hw** in **wh**ich; ri**ng**; **sh**op; **th**in; **th**ere; **zh** in trea**s**ure.

top hat (top´ hat´) *n.* A man's hat that has a tall top shaped like a tube.

toppled (to´ pəld) *adj.* Overturned.

transform (trans´ form) *v.* To change outward appearance.

trout (trout) *n.* A long bony fish.

trudge (truj) *v.* To walk with great effort.

tutoring (too´ tər ing) *n.* Helping others with school work.

twitch (twich) *v.* To move with a jerk.

U

unaware (ən´ ə wâr´) *adv.* Not knowing what is happening.

unusual (un ū´ zhoo əl) *adj.* Not usual, common, or ordinary; rare.

W

wakeful (wāk´ fəl) *adj.* Restless, not able to sleep.

wand (wond) *n.* A magic rod; a stick that is used for magic.

wariest (wâr´ ē əst) *adj.* Superlative of **wary:** Having a feeling that danger may be near; watching for danger.

watchman (woch´ mən) *n.* A man whose job is to guard property.

waterspout (wô´ tər spout´) *n.* A stream of water that shoots from a whale's blowhole when it comes to the surface for air.

wedged (wejd) *v.* To drive, push, or crowd.

whir (hwûr) *v.* To fly quickly, making a noise with wings.

whirlwind (hwûrl´ wind´) *n.* Wind that moves in a circle with great force.

wily (wī´ lē) *adj.* Sly or crafty.

Y

yip (yip) *v.* To make a short high-pitched sound.

Photo Credits

11, ©Tom & Pat Leeson/DRK Photo; **22 (t),** file photo, **(b)** ©SYS, Japan; **80,** Albert Whitman Company; **82,** The National Museum of American Art, Smithsonian Institution, Washinton, DC. Gift of S.C. Johnson & Son, Inc./ Art Resource, NY; **83 (t),** Christie's Images, **(b)** The Metropolitan Museum of Art, Arthur Hoppock Hearn Fund, 1913. Photograph ©1988 The Metropolitan Museum of Art; **104 (t),** ©Arte Publico Press, **(b)** ©Bernd Noble; **118 (t),** file photo, **(b)** Jose Aruego; **136 (t),** Scholastic, **(b)** file photo; **154, 176,** file photo; **178,** The Metropolitan Museum of Art, Rogers Fund, 1930. Photograph ©1979 The Metropolitan Museum of Art; **179 (t),** University of Pennsylvania Museum, Philadelphia, neg # T4-171c, **(b)** The Museum of Fine Arts, Houston; The John A. and Audrey Jones Beck Collection; **196,** file photo; **220,** The Times; **234 (t),** Adri Coen, **(b)** Lane Yerkes; **250,** Scholastic; **264 (t),** Craig Kee Strete, **(b)** Jose Aruego; **294,** The Norton Simon Foundation, Pasadena, California; **295 (t),** ©Tom Amedis, **(b)** The National Museum of Women in the Arts, Washington, DC. Gift of Deidre Busenberg and the Artist; **332,** Barbara Knutson; **334,** Darrell Gulin/DRK Photo; **335,** Tom Till/DRK Photo; **336,** Fred Bruemmer/DRK Photo; **337,** ©M.C. Chamberlain/DRK Photo; **338,** James P. Rowan/DRK Photo; **339,** ©Tom & Pat Leeson/DRK Photo; **340,** Andy Rouse/DRK Photo; **341,** Pat & Tom Leeson/Photo Researchers, Inc.; **342,** C.C. Lockwood/Animals Animals; **343,** Larry Mishkar/Dembinsky Photo Associates; **344,** Rod Planck/ Photo Researchers, Inc.; **345,** Wayne Lankinen/DRK Photo; **346,** Stan Wayman/Photo Researchers, Inc.; **347,** Leonard Lee Rue III//DRK Photo; **348,** Wayne Lankinen/DRK Photo; **349,** Gary R. Zahm/DRK Photo; **350,** Gilbert S. Grant/Photo Researchers, Inc.; **351,** Joe McDonald/DRK Photo; **352,** M.H. Sharp/Photo Researchers, Inc.; **353,** Ray Coleman/Photo Researchers, Inc.; **354,** Bruce Watkins/Animals Animals; **355,** Tom McHugh/Photo Researchers, Inc.; **356,** John Bova/Photo Researchers, Inc.; **357,** David M. Schleser/Photo Researchers, Inc.; **358,** Janet McDonnell.

Art Acknowledgments

Unit 1 (Sharing Stories) Bill Ogden
Unit 2 (Kindness) Sucie Stevenson
Unit 3 (Look Again) Dara Goldman